CHILLIN
FROM REA
PRESENT-DAY EXPERIENCES OF THE PARANORMAL

CHILLING TALES
FROM DERBYSHIRE

PRESENT-DAY EXPERIENCES OF THE PARANORMAL

NETTY

breedon **books**
PUBLISHING

First published in Great Britain in 2009 by
The Breedon Books Publishing Company Limited
Breedon House, 3 The Parker Centre, Derby, DE21 4SZ.

ISBN   978-1-85983-687-3
Printed and bound TJ International Ltd, Padstow, Cornwall.

CONTENTS

For Leeky, Jack, Hannah, Olivia & Twinkle

THANKS

Firstly, I would like to thank the people of Derbyshire and everyone who has contributed their personal experiences and given their permission for me to share them.

Also to the BBC, the *Derby Evening Telegraph* and local media who have interviewed me and helped collate some of the stories in this book.

Thank you to my husband, Leeky, for your help with researching the stories that I have been sent for use in this book and for your love and support.

To my three children, Jack, Hannah and Olivia, a huge thank you for being you and for putting up with me. Special thanks must also go to Mum, Dad, Andrew, Heather, Paul, Lynda, Nana Eunice, Grandad Harry, Lorraine, Mark, Lynette and Tony for their constant support.

DISCLAIMER

Neither the author nor the publisher can guarantee the authenticity of the stories that have been submitted and included in this book. They have been included and accepted in good faith. The witness account of events have been published as described first-hand to the author and have not been altered in any way other than for ease of understanding. The identity of the witness has been protected as requested when submitting their account for inclusion in the book.

FOREWORD

My first encounter with a ghost happened when I was a very young child and living with my parents, brother Andrew and sister Heather in Ockbrook, Derbyshire.

Our home was a new build set in the corner of a cul-de-sac in a modern estate. It was quite an impressive house, with a long driveway, and had all the latest mod cons. It was built on the site of a former farm and to me it always had an eerie feel about it.

In the 1970s everyone's telephone number was in the phone book, and my family were no exception, but every year when the new directory was delivered it would always give our address as 'Yew Tree Farm'. Year after year my parents told BT about the address, but still it was never corrected.

I was born at home, so you might think that I would have fond memories of my birthplace, but I can honestly say that I never felt at ease there, refusing to go upstairs on my own and running past any windows without looking into them for fear of what I might see.

The dining room was, to me, the worst room in the house. It had a large window overlooking the driveway and the most horrendous chill, despite the rest of the house baking in the heat from the central heating. No radiator could ever heat that room up, and I remember thinking that the old man in the corner, looking out of the window and smoking a pipe, must have been very cold in there.

I can remember the man clearly as he sat in a chair, wearing his flat cap and grey cardigan. He never spoke and just puffed away on his pipe. His skin was very grey and he had a bluish hue about his body. I was the only one who could see him, but other members of my family had commented on smelling his pipe tobacco.

I knew he was not friendly and I always remember thinking that he did not want me there. If my mum ever asked me to go into that room I would say the 'Hail Mary' prayer in my head over and over again until I felt safe again. I was not sure if the Virgin Mary was listening to me, but I guessed that she must be close by as my mum used to tell me off for whistling because it made the Virgin Mary blush!

Strange faces would also appear on top of the wardrobe and I could see Roman soldiers marching into the bottom of the stairs, disappearing at knee level. Light bulbs would blow and then relight, then go off again without explanation, and our dog would growl fearlessly, hairs standing on end, at something outside, but nothing was there. I also feared the dark and slept with the light on, making any excuse to go down to the safety of my parents in the lounge.

The worst part about living in the house was that I knew when I was going to see or experience something as I would hear the strangest mechanical sound in both ears, which would grow louder and louder just before I witnessed anything paranormal.

To the rest of the family I had an overactive, vivid imagination and was destined to be on the stage, but to me it was very real and I did not understand what the things I was seeing were or how to make them go away.

It was not until I was at primary school, when a boy showed me a picture of a ghost book with real photographs of ghosts in, that I realised nobody else could see the Roman soldiers or the old man smoking his pipe because they were ghosts. Maybe the old man was the ghost of the farmer wanting to claim back his land, which would explain why it was always listed as 'Yew Tree Farm'. The thought terrified me, and little did I know then that I would end up with a career in which the majority of my colleagues could be described as non-living. And do you know what? I still sleep with the light on!

CHAPTER 1

GHOST STORIES

SO WHAT IS A GHOST?

If I had a pound for every time I have been asked this question then I would probably be sitting on a beach somewhere sipping cocktails. Yet when you actually stop and think about the question it is clear you have to delve deep in order to get the answer.

Often the things that we call 'ghosts' are not ghosts in the true sense of the word and this can lead to confusion. According to the Oxford English Dictionary, the word ghost means: an apparition of a dead person which is believed to appear to the living. The truth is many people do not understand what is meant by the term. Also, if you factor into an encounter the witness's own state of mind, surroundings and belief system, you cannot rule out the possibility that they have jumped to conclusions or have an overactive imagination.

So what is a ghost and, further, what distinguishes them from those other manifestations of the paranormal realm? In other words, what are the main features which allow you to say that it is a 'true ghost'? While this is a subject that will always cause a heated debate, my own experiences and those of well-known mediums and researchers who I have worked with have led me to the conclusion that a true ghost has three distinct traits which stand them apart from other paranormal existences. This is obviously not conclusive and the study of the paranormal is not an exact science; it makes research and findings rather subjective, but to me that only adds to the fun.

SO WHAT ARE THE THREE TRAITS OF A 'TRUE GHOST'?

A true ghost is always human, or, to be accurate in my explanation, the ghost is the disembodied conscious energy of a once living person. This means that for whatever reason (one we will probably never fully understand) some people leave their physical body to decay when they die and remain in a spiritual state on the physical plane.

Many people mistake angels and other supernatural entities for ghosts, but these are celestials and have never been human or existed in the physical state. This point is important to remember as the very nature of the entity may allow you to shed some light on the purpose and nature of the sighting and what the entity can and cannot do with the boundaries of linear time, space and the laws of physics.

The second trait of a true ghost is that it is interactive, to some degree. It has the ability to manipulate matter, seemingly observe its surroundings and be observed either by the naked eye or by use of electronic capturing devices. Now, before you cry out that the same could be said for spirit guides, residual entities or poltergeists – it is indeed especially true for poltergeists – this does suggest that some of these could potentially be ghosts, but such apparitions are usually just manifestations of conscious energy and not ghosts in their own right, just because the entity is interactive does not necessarily mean that it has had a human existence. Also entities which appear human but do not interact are nothing more than a conscious energy replay – an event recorded within the environment – and are not true ghosts either.

The third characteristic is unique to ghosts as they are not naturally part of the spiritual realms but beings that exist parallel to both the spiritual and physical worlds and have influences in both.

I believe that ghosts are beings which are unnaturally confined to the physical realm for a variety of reasons, usually to do with either a free-will decision to stay behind or an unwillingness to completely move on to the next level of existence. In essence, then, depending upon your point of view, ghosts are either 'trapped' or choose to reside in a type of twilight state that exists between the spiritual and physical realms, effectively making them residents of neither the physical nor the spiritual realm.

I personally do not believe that being a ghost is a particularly good position to be in as I strongly believe that we are spiritual beings who exist within the confines of a physical body for a reason, and to be trapped between these worlds is to exist in an unnatural state that can be frightening and unpleasant for those caught in it and positively terrifying for those unaware of what is going on.

New Age teaching teaches the fact that the soul immediately moves into the spiritual realm upon death. This idea is challenged by the possible existence of ghosts – human consciousnesses caught between the two worlds. However, there is no contradiction when we understand that what is caught in this transitional no man's land is not the human soul (the soul effortlessly transcends this zone upon death or birth) but the individual personality that soul has generated.

In essence, a ghost is the flotsam of the soul, the ego of a previous incarnation that has essentially detached itself from its resident soul and has been cast adrift in the twilight zone between the spiritual and physical realms. That is why it can continue to haunt for decades or even centuries when the soul that generated it has long-since moved on.

SO WHY DOES A GHOST CHOOSE TO STAY ON THE PHYSICAL PLANE AND HOW DOES IT EVER MOVE ON FROM THAT STATE?

I believe that it would choose to stay for a number of reasons. Firstly, it may be attached to something or someone in the physical realm and simply refuses to give them up. This can happen when a family member simply cannot bare to be parted from their loved ones. Secondly, the ghost may be too traumatised by their own death to move on. This can happen when the physical death is fast and tragic, like in a car crash. The spirit does not have time to prepare for its own death and is expelled at speed from the physical body. It is a case of 'Where the hell am I? What's happened?'

Sometimes the ghost will not move on for fear of judgement, especially if they have not lived a very honest life, or may become trapped because they are anchored to the physical realm by great rage and are unwilling to let go of that anger.

So, how does a ghost move on? Many move on of their own accord when they become tired; however, some need help, either from sympathetic humans willing to convince the entity of the futility of remaining behind (or, in the case of mission or goodbye ghosts, giving it 'permission' to go) or from spiritual entities on the other side whose task it is to show these lost personalities the way out. Just as free-will can determine whether one becomes a ghost in the first place, it seems it can also have a hand in determining how long a ghost will remain.

The universe is extremely respectful of our decisions, even if those decisions result in us experiencing unnecessary anguish and pain (in death as well as in life). In effect, it really is all up to us, whether we realise it or not.

Therefore, I believe that many humans will never become a ghost because most will move on to the spiritual realm quickly and naturally, as their spirit was designed to do, stopping off at the acclimation realm to reflect on their life and make decisions on their future regarding the spiritual lessons they need to learn.

Obviously, you may have your own religious and spiritual beliefs and I totally respect each and every belief system. The wonderful thing about paranormal and spiritual experiences is that at the very essence of belief is what you, the witness, perceive to be true, and for that I am truly grateful as it makes all our experiences and encounters totally unique.

Therefore, I have no doubt that the accounts which have been told to me in this book are true, or as true as the witness believes them to be.

Happy reading!

I'M THE BOSS! - DERBY

We purchased our house in an auction and so we never got to meet the previous owners. It needed a lot of work, but we got it for a song and therefore considered the investment worthwhile, even if my wife and I had to bring in a team of builders to complete the work – I was definitely not the DIY type and we both worked full-time.

We scouted around for competent builders and came across a man called Dave who ran his own small building company. Although he was not the cheapest, he seemed to have vast experience so we decided to offer him the work.

Dave arrived nice and early and I met him to hand over the keys and explain which part of the job we wanted doing first before heading off to my office.

On my way home I decided to call in to see how Dave was getting on. He was upstairs ripping out the bathroom when I arrived, and so I went straight upstairs to see how he was.

'Things are going fine,' he said. 'Although, if you could have a word with the old man and ask him to stop coming into the bathroom when I'm working I would really appreciate it. He doesn't say anything, he just stands there watching me and it is kind of off-putting.'

'What old man?' I asked, puzzled. 'The house is empty.'

Dave continued: 'Don't be daft. I saw him with my own eyes. He was about 70 years old and just stood there nodding at me. All the doors were locked. I assumed he was related to you.'

I spent the next hour convincing Dave that there was nobody in the house before we both left for the night.

When I was locking the house I saw a neighbour and felt compelled to ask her who had lived in the house previously. She told me that a builder had lived there all his life. He had been born in the house and remained there until his dying day.

Dave saw the old man a lot throughout the project, and each time he just stood there nodding. I am convinced that he was the ghost of the old builder, keeping a watchful eye on the building work and his beloved house.

THE GHOST CYCLIST - SPONDON

In 2003 my friend and I were on our way home from a pleasant evening of playing snooker in Spondon. It was raining heavily, so driving conditions along Dale Road were treacherous as the rain pelted on the windscreen.

In front of us I saw a cyclist and can clearly remember feeling pity for him as all he was wearing was a blue jumper, a white flat cap and cream summer trousers. He had no protection from the violent storm that was pounding him on his red bike.

We passed Bartlewood Lodge and the cyclist was riding a few yards in front of us. He followed a bend in the road, so I alerted my friend to warn him not to take the corner too fast. My friend told me not to worry as he had already seen him and we discussed how lucky we were to be in a car and the fact that the cyclist would be like a drowned rat by the time he got home.

We rounded the corner and once again the cyclist was just in front of us, and my friend decided that it would now be safe to overtake him as his speed was starting to drop. We overtook the cyclist slowly and both kept an eye on the rider to ensure he had enough room as we passed.

As we drove parallel to him, we both noticed that we could see right through him and his bike. He disappeared before our very eyes and it seemed like we were looking through a bluish, see-through haze. We both panicked as we discussed what we had just witnessed. The hairs on the back of my neck stood on end as we concluded that there were no turnings off the road at that point and we had both been watching him as we overtook. There was no possible explanation as to how he had simply vanished and I wanted to get back to the safety of my home fast.

I did not tell too many people what I had witnessed that night for fear of being ridiculed. However, about two weeks later I was talking to another friend, Paul, in a pub and simply asked if he believed in ghosts. He told me that he had not done, until the day when he was driving home from work along Dale Road and saw a cyclist who disappeared before his very eyes. A chill went down my spine as I asked him to describe what the cyclist was wearing and what happened. I had not mentioned my own sighting of the ghost cyclist but my friend Paul was giving a detailed account of what he had seen and it was identical to what I had previously witnessed myself.

ANOTHER SIGHTING OF THE CYCLIST – SPONDON

My wife and I had enjoyed a meal to celebrate our wedding anniversary at Bartlewood Lodge and later returned to the car to commence our journey home. The weather was particularly bad that night and I was looking forward to getting home to our house in Stanley Common.

As I approached the junction to turn onto Dale Road, my wife asked me if I had seen the cyclist who had just passed and I replied that I had and thought he must be a bloody idiot for riding on a night like this without any lights.

As I turned onto Dale Road, I saw the bike in front and decided to overtake him before the road started to bend, but as I approached him he disappeared. However, we had clearly seen him moments before in a blue jumper and white cap. We could not believe what we had seen.

THE MOTORCYCLIST – SMALLEY

It was 4 November 2006 and the time was five past eight in the evening. I can be so precise because my family and I were travelling back from my parents' house in Spondon along Morley Road and I had just checked the time on the clock in the car. As we approached Smalley crossroads, the lights turned to red so I slowed down and came to a stop, waiting for the traffic lights to change. I sat patiently, staring ahead, when all of a sudden I saw an outline of a motorbike lying in the middle of the road. Then, all of a sudden, I saw the ghost of a man wearing a helmet get up from the road and walk towards the pavement near the motorbike shop on the corner. As he walked towards me, I could see straight through him, and all the hairs on the back of my neck stood on end.

Not wanting to scare my children, I decided not to say anything, but suddenly my son shouted loudly, 'I think I have just seen a ghost wearing a helmet!' Then my husband and daughter said that they had seen it too. When the lights changed we drove straight over the ghostly motorbike and the air in the car had a real chill about it as we passed through.

We often spoke about the ghost when we approached the crossroads but didn't see him again until a year to the day of our first sighting. Once again we found ourselves waiting at a red light, and when I glanced at the clock I noticed it was exactly the same time as it had been when we travelled that road the previous year. To our amazement the ghostly figure once again rose from the road and walked to the pavement.

I have tried searching the internet for crashes involving a motorbike on that stretch of road but as yet I have not been able to find any information.

THE GHOST COACH – GUILDHALL, DERBY

I never believed in ghosts until the summer of 1980 when my fiancé and I saw something that frightened us to our very core and will stay with us for the rest of our lives.

We had been shopping in Derby, buying my birthday presents, and decided that as it was such a nice day we would go for something to eat and then stay on in Derby for a few drinks.

We walked around Iron Gate and were crossing the market place towards the entrance to the Guildhall, when all of a sudden we heard the sound of horses' hooves. The noise was deafening. We stopped in our tracks to see where the sound was coming from, but we could not see anything out of place so continued walking forward. Then out of nowhere we saw what can only be described as a ghostly horse-drawn coach pull up near the archway to the Guildhall. Although we could see it, we could also see through it, and my fiancé and I stood staring, rooted to the spot. It was about 8ft high and was being pulled by four ghostly horses. Then, as fast as it had appeared, the coach and horses disappeared into thin air.

My fiancé and I could not believe what we had just seen, and thankfully I have never seen a ghost since. Now, every time I am near the entrance to the Guildhall I quicken my step, not wanting another ghostly encounter.

REMOTE VIEWING – HEANOR

Having lived on High Street, Heanor, for many years, I had never experienced anything that I could call paranormal before. The road on which I lived was the main road so it always had a steady flow of traffic going up and down and the sounds of police sirens often filled the air.

After a hard day at work I could not wait to get into my bed, but as I did so I found that, try as I might, I simply could not get to sleep, due to the noise of the traffic and the sirens whizzing past. I decided to watch a bit of television in the hope that it would tire me enough so I could finally get to sleep.

I lay in bed watching television and became engrossed in the programme. The door to the bedroom was firmly shut and there was nobody else in the house as I lived alone, but all of a sudden I saw a tall black figure float through my bedroom door. It was a solid mass and about 6ft tall, and the sight of it frightened the living daylights out of me. I could not have spoken or moved if I tried.

As I watched, the figure floated across my bedroom and then seemed to hover for a few minutes in front of the television, then turn it off before floating back towards the closed bedroom door and through it.

To this day, I have no idea what it was and there is no logical explanation other than it must have been a ghost.

I have seen it several times since and each time it floats across and turns off the television, so maybe it doesn't like my choice of programme!

THE LADY IN BLUE – KEDLESTON HALL

In the summer of 1997, my cousins came over from Canada to stay with us and I wanted to make their stay as memorable as possible as they had never visit Derbyshire before. We had glorious days in the Peak District and had just about exhausted the credit cards on various shopping trips, so on the Sunday we decided to have a picnic at Kedleston Hall.

After arriving at the hall we set off to explore the beautiful gardens and landscape. As we were doing so my cousin pointed to a lady wearing a beautiful crinoline dress. She was standing still and seemed to be admiring the beautiful landscape too. I told my cousin that I thought she must be an extra in a period drama as many of the old stately homes were used for filming. So we decided to ask her what film she was in. As we approached her we could see that she was wearing a beautiful lace hat and she looked so pretty, but when we got to about 4ft away from her she turned to face us then simply disappeared.

My cousin and I could not believe what we had just witnessed, so we decided to find a member of staff to ask if they had any ideas about who the lady was.

We walked back to the house and found ourselves chatting like excitable children as we explained to a gentleman what we had just seen. He told us that he too had seen this woman on many occasions and believed that she once lived in the hall.

I have visited the hall again many times, but to this day I have never seen the beautiful woman again, and I feel really privileged that she showed herself to us on that day.

THE DARE – FRIARGATE HOUSE SCHOOL

I attended Friargate House School as a boarder and loved every minute of my time there. The school was very grand and still had many of its original features, from ornate toilets to the servants' staircases which ran up to the many floors of the building.

The high ceilings and original windows made my friends and I feel like the school was our stately home, and we used to spend many hours after the school day had finished pretending that we were princesses. We used to get the less popular pupils to pretend that they were our servants, while I always played the best parts.

One night, after playing such a game, we decided to have a game of dare. This was not an easy task because the staff members ruled with a rod of iron and you would certainly get a lashing of their tongue if they found you out of bed past bedtime. This just added to the excitement, though, and so my friends and I drew straws to see who would do the first dare.

It was not my lucky night as I had drawn the shortest straw, so my friends huddled together to decide my fate. My dare was to go downstairs and ring the old hand bell then run back to bed without being detected.

Seizing my chance, I tiptoed down the staircase without making a sound, found the bell, rang it and then ran like the wind back into my bed. Within seconds a staff member was standing in our dorm as we all pretended to be asleep. I lay still, trying to stifle my giggles and feeling immense pride because I had completed my mission.

When it was safe to come out of our beds, my friends and I got out the straws to see who would be next to complete a dare; it was my friend June's turn, and as I had completed the first dare I had to choose her task. I decided that she had to go down into the basement and bring back a pair of plimsolls that the day children wore. The basement was not the friendliest of places in the school as it had very little lighting and had a strange smell about it, and to be honest none of us enjoyed being in that part of the school.

Not wanting to be seen as a sissy, June reluctantly crept out of our dorm and went on her mission. She seemed to be gone for ages – far longer than it would have taken to go down the two flights of stairs – and eventually we assumed she must have been caught. After half an hour we were all getting anxious, so my friend Anna and I decided that we would try and find her, and would use the story that Anna felt sick if a member of staff caught us.

We sneaked down the stairs undetected and crept down the narrow servants' stairs into the basement. There we found June crying in a corner, and her face as white as a sheet. She was so scared that she could not speak and simply pointed to a window. We both looked to where she was pointing and could clearly see the ghost of a little boy peering through the window. There was no mistake that it was a ghost as he was almost transparent but had a blue hue about him. He looked about eight years old and stood looking straight at us.

My two friends and I scarpered from the basement and ran straight into the arms of a member of staff. I told her that June and Anna were not feeling well – and she must have taken pity on us as we certainly did not look right – as we did not want to tell her what we had seen in the basement because we would have been in big trouble. She certainly would not have believed our story so we would have been scolded for lying as well, even though the three of us were convinced that we had seen a ghost.

We never played dare again for fear of seeing the ghost boy and thankfully we never had any other encounters during our time at the school.

THE GHOST JUMPER – BORROWASH

My friend Alan and I were up early one day to go on a bike ride to the River Derwent and do a spot of fishing. It was a crisp morning, and as we set off from our homes in Chellaston we rode the familiar path past Elvaston Castle towards Borrowash.

We soon approached the bridge over the river and dismounted our bikes as we turned off the road and onto the grassy bank along the Derwent, chatting about where would be a good spot to fish that day.

We found a spot and soon settled down. Although it was still early in the day, the excitement and journey had made us hungry so we sat and ate our packed lunches, which my mum had kindly made for us. As we were enjoying our food, it suddenly went deathly silent, you could not hear a bird in the sky, and it seemed that the whole world stood still for those few seconds. The only thing I can liken it to is the strange air I experienced when I saw a full eclipse of the sun years later, and anyone who has witnessed an eclipse will know what I am talking about.

Just as Alan and I were nervously commenting that something did not feel right, he suddenly pointed to the footbridge. I looked and could clearly see a woman in full period dress balancing on the edge of the bridge, looking like she was ready to jump.

Alan and I got to our feet and started running towards the woman, but before we could get close enough to stop her she jumped, and as she did so she disappeared before our eyes. There was no 'splash' sound, as you would expect if someone had jumped in, and on inspection of the river there was no sign of her. We were sure that she had vanished just as she jumped and had not actually hit the water.

We stood there in disbelief, revelling in the fact that we had seen a ghost, when suddenly the lady reappeared on the bridge and repeated the same action of jumping off and disappearing. On seeing her for the second time, Alan and I grabbed our things, jumped on our bikes and rode back to the safety of our homes as fast as we could.

On returning home we both ran into my house and told my dad what we have seen, only to be told off for lying! It was at that point Alan and I decided we would have to be very selective over who we told the story to, but as you can imagine it has become a firm favourite at Halloween parties.

CRY IN THE NIGHT – BRADLEY

Since my retirement I have been able to indulge in one of my favourite pastimes: walking in the Derbyshire Dales. I really believe it is God's own county, and I have worked hard throughout my career so I can now take off for weeks on end in Derbyshire, just me and my tent.

In September 2007 I was packed and ready to go to Bradley, a small village near Ashbourne, on the first part of an expedition. I arrived at the campsite at around 3pm and soon had my tent up, so I decided to walk into the village for something to eat and some liquid refreshment.

I had never visited Bradley before and was keen to sample the goods at the local pub, which is famous for having two names; it is either The Jinglers or The Fox and Hounds, depending on which way you are travelling, and I was intrigued to find out why the pub was named so.

The atmosphere inside was lovely and the locals were more than happy to welcome me as their guest as we drank away the hours, telling some of the tales and stories of Derbyshire. It was starting to get dark when I left the pub, and although I was definitely not drunk I would be lying if I said that I was totally sober. I would like to point out, though, that I could walk in a straight line and was more than capable of walking the distance to the campsite.

As I walked through the village I heard 'Mary! Mary!' being shouted out by a man followed by the thunderous sound of horses' hooves, and I can remember standing close into the stone wall so that the horses could pass – but I could see nothing.

I continued walking through the village and saw what I can only describe as the ghosts of two men arguing next to a building which had a hole in the wall. The men were dressed very grandly and I could clearly hear the name 'Hugo' being shouted, and then the two ghosts disappeared. What I saw had the most amazing sobering effect on me, and within seconds I was on full alert, but as I sobered up fear set in and I ran the rest of the way back.

I continued travelling for the next week, but on my return I visited the library to see if I could shed any light on what I had seen in Bradley. I soon found what I was looking for – apparently a man called Hugo built the hall in Bradley and he had a sister called Mary. Could I have been a witness to a scene from the past?

THE GHOSTLY FUNERAL PROCESSION AT THE OLD SILK MILL - DERBY

When I was a little girl, growing up behind the Old Silk Mill in Derby, I would often hear the sound of horses and carts coming from the cobbled street below my bedroom.

I shared my bedroom with six brothers and sisters, with the girls at one end of the bed and the boys at the other, and we would often lie in bed listening out for the sounds of the horses and making up stories about them.

One night we were particularly excited and were having trouble getting off to sleep, when all of a sudden we heard the sound of horses' hooves outside, but this time we could all clearly hear music being played. We all dashed out of bed, ran to the window and saw what can only be described as a ghostly funeral procession marching up the street.

We all screamed and ran into my parents' room to tell them what we had seen. I am not sure if they believed us, but for a few days my parents let us all sleep on their bedroom floor.

AMEN ALLEY - DERBY

My eldest brother Ernest and I used to play marbles along Amen Alley in Derby. It was by far our favourite game. I loved spending time with my big brother and he always had the best marbles.

One day, we were playing in the alley when my brother suddenly froze to the spot. His face looked as white as a sheet and he started to stammer.

'What's the matter Ernest?' I enquired.

'There's a bloody nun behind you and she is hovering with no bloody feet!' He replied, clearly distressed.

I immediately turned around but saw nothing and teased Ernest that maybe he was going mad.

'I ain't mad!' He shouted. 'It's bloody standing over you. 'Tis you who is mad, 'cause you ain't seen it!' Then, quick as a flash, he ran home, leaving me standing there in the middle of Amen Alley with a nun that I could not see.

Ernest has been dead for many years, but of all the stories about him this is my favourite, as I never again saw my big brother looking that scared.

THE FIRE GIRL – HEANOR

My husband and I were visiting Heanor Antiques Centre one Saturday. We were browsing through the shelves when all of a sudden my husband felt a slight tug at his jacket. He immediately looked down to see what it was and to his horror saw the ghost of a little girl with blonde straggly hair and blackened features. Her hands seemed to be nothing more than stubs. My husband shouted my name and the little girl vanished.

Clearly shocked by the experience, my husband wanted to leave and go home, and I knew that he was telling the truth as he was not superstitious and nor was he the sort of person to make things up. However, I was intrigued by what had happened to him and wanted to stay to see if the little girl would reappear, but she did not and so we made our way out of the shop. We stopped to look at something that had caught my eye in the window, and we were still talking about the little girl my husband had seen when an elderly lady, who was also looking in the window, stopped us as she had overheard some of our conversation.

The old lady told us that the little girl had been seen on many occasions and had once lived in the building. One day, she had been drying her dolly's clothes in front of the fire when her own dress was set alight causing a major fire in the building and killing the little girl.

LONG-LOST LOVERS AT SWARKESTONE BRIDGE? – DERBY

Many years ago I worked at the Crewe and Harper pub near Swarkestone Bridge in Derby, which is steeped in history.

On my first day there, a local told me the story of the bridge and how legend has it that it was paid for by two sisters who each lost the love of their life in the river. Although I had heard the story before, the way that this local told it to me suddenly made it all seem real, and I felt a strange sense of emotion wash over me at the thought that the two young men had drowned trying to see their fair maidens. I soon forgot about the story, though, and carried on with my work as it was a busy night and I wanted to show my new bosses that I was more than up to the job. The end of my shift approached so I put on my coat and went to see my boss, as instructed. Just then, as we were talking, we saw strange lights through the window near the river and my boss said that we had to investigate in case it was someone messing around in the water or planning to break into the pub. So we ran around the side of the building towards the river.

We could clearly see the lights now, and they seemed to be darting just above the water. They were round and white, and as there was no moon that night they could not have been a reflection. Then we heard what I can only describe as a terrifying scream that did not sound human, and one of the lights seemed to be moving frantically towards the other one and then darting back again. Then they disappeared into the water and the air was still.

When we returned to the pub, my boss said that he was sure what we had seen were orbs, and I asked if he thought they could have been the spirits of the lovers that were lost. He did not think that they were as he had heard they drowned further down the river where the bridge now stands, so he suggested they could be the spirits of other people.

I continued to work at the pub for many years, but I would never travel alone after my shift and I was scared to look out of the window just in case I saw the orbs again.

RESTLESS SPIRITS – DERBY

One day I was in my bedroom with some friends. Suddenly we heard a big bang and all rushed downstairs. I cried 'Mum, is that you?' but she had gone out with my dad. We told ourselves that it was nothing and went back upstairs just a little confused. Then we heard a smash in the living room and ran down again. We were confronted by magazines and glasses flying around the room. We screamed like hell and ran to our neighbour's house where we waited for my parents to return.

Every night afterwards whatever it was came back and smashed things or made them fly across the room. We were terrified and my mum asked the salesman at the show home in Hilton about the house, but he could not tell us anything about the property or the land it was built on to help solve the problem.

The phenomenon got worse. It turned lights on and off and even scratched my dad down his back. Eventually things got too much for my family and we moved out. I have never seen anything like that since, thank goodness.

INCEY-WINCEY SPIDER - OAKWOOD

For some reason whenever I was in my garden I heard the nursery rhyme *The Incey-wincey Spider* being sung by a little girl. Although I never saw her, I always heard her singing the same rhyme as I hung out my washing, and I presumed that it was the daughter of my new neighbours who I had yet to meet but had moved in several months earlier.

One day I went back outside to fetch the washing in and heard the same rhyme being sung again, so I sneaked towards the fence dividing our gardens and peeked over to see if I could see the child, but nobody was there.

Several days later, when I was coming out of the house at the same time as my new neighbour, we stopped to introduce ourselves. Wanting to seem polite, I told her I often heard her daughter singing *Incey-wincey Spider* in the garden and that I thought she had a beautiful voice. My neighbour's face started to crumple and tears started to flow from her eyes.

'My daughter died from meningitis three years ago; she was four years old when she died and that was her favourite nursery rhyme,' she sobbed, and soon I found myself crying with her.

I never heard the little girl again, and I strongly believe her spirit needed to let her mum know that she was OK and had moved home with her. I know after speaking to my neighbour again that when she had time to take in what had happened on our first meeting, she felt comforted and safe that her child had never really left her.

HAUNTED HOUSE - DERBY

When I was a child we lived in a maisonette in a Victorian terraced house in the west end of Derby. The house was very typical of the area, and our flat occupied what would have been the basement or servants' quarters (we know this because when our old floorboards were treated for woodworm a system of servant-summoning bells were found) and the old ground floor (which included the front door, entranceway, reception room, front room and kitchen). The upper two floors were converted into a separate flat, which was occupied by members of my extended family.

Our flat had a horrible feeling to it, an atmosphere not shared by the upper flat. There was a gloominess that could not simply be attributed to the flat being situated in the basement. Throughout our childhood, my sister (who is five years older) and I experienced frequent terrifying events.

The two main areas where events occurred were the staircase from the ground floor to the basement and the front bedroom of the house. The basement itself had an uneasy feeling about it and my sister and I would avoid playing or being alone down there as much as we could.

It was almost as if there was someone constantly behind you, watching you. My sister and I always used to run up the stairs in fear. When you got to about the third or fourth step it felt as if someone was trying to grab you or touch you on the back, a feeling similar to when someone pulls you by the shirt. Also, when descending from the top of the stairs we often felt as if we were being touched or followed.

Sometimes we felt a cold gust of air go past, as if someone was running past. We both also caught glimpses, out of the corner of our eyes, of a dark shape following us up and down the stairs. Whatever the presence was, it was definitely malevolent and wanted to make its existence known. My parents also sometimes felt as if they were being watched or followed but not as intensely as me or my sister.

One night, when I was about six, my mother found me screaming, lying at bottom of the stairs with a sprained ankle. At the time I remember feeling as if I had been dropped, but I have no recollection of how I got there. I admit I could have been sleepwalking and fallen, but I had no past history of this and it has not happened since.

The presence on the stairs, however, was nothing compared to what we experienced in the front bedroom. When I was very small my parents occupied this room and I had a little bed there too. I distinctly remember being woken up one night by the sound of somebody singing. I opened my eyes and saw three children dressed in white, dancing around in a circle, as though they were playing 'ring-a-ring-o'-roses'. Although the apparition was not sinister it was enough to scare me. I closed my eyes tightly and the singing stopped, but when I opened them again I clearly saw the figure of a little boy, probably about five or six years old with sandy blond hair, wearing what looked like a choirboy gown (but it could have been a victorian-style nightgown), standing at the end of my bed, watching me. He watched me for a couple of minutes, which felt like hours, before he disappeared. I was only about three or four myself when this happened but I remember the events so vividly that I am 100 per cent sure it was not a dream.

When I was a little older my sister took residence in the same room. One night, as she was listening to music, something caught her eye, and when she looked up she saw the horrifying figure of a wizened old man walking past her doorway. She said he was quite short, with a horrible face and white hair. He stopped, glared at her menacingly and then disappeared. I can remember the night it happened because my poor sister came running up the stairs screaming and did not calm down for several days.

Some time later, in the same room, she said that she felt an oppressive feeling of being watched while she got dressed. As she looked around her room to see if anyone was there, she caught sight of a blonde girl glaring at her from the mirror. The girl's face was apparently quite contorted and she appeared to be very angry. Once again my sister fled in fear. The room had the same feeling to it as the staircase. It was also always freezing no matter how high the heating was turned up and regardless of the time of year.

Some very strange things happened in that flat. All of us heard singing and snatches of whispered conversations. The radio, TV and washing machine would turn themselves off and on. It was not uncommon to come home and find all of these things switched on, when no one had been into the flat. Because it happened so frequently, my mother made a point of never leaving anything on standby so that it could not be attributed to faulty electrics. Thankfully we moved out of there when I was a young teenager.

The family who moved in after us were so convinced by the tales of what we had experienced that they got their local priest to come and give the house a full blessing before they moved in. They subsequently have not shared any of our experiences.

I know that all of the things I have reported seem extraordinary, but I felt compelled to share them after reading other people's accounts of experiences they have had.

I would like to point out that in adulthood I am training to be a cognitive psychologist and am fully aware of all the 'scientific explanations' that could be used for what my sister and I experienced. I am, however, convinced that what we encountered was very real and supernatural.

HAPPY HALLOWEEN – DERBY

During the family Halloween party two years ago my grandparents, mother and stepfather decided to scare my younger sister and I by telling us their stories about the ghost in the house. They also described how, when we were too young to understand, we used to complain that when we spent the night at our grandparents' house the dog would jump on our bed at night, when in fact our grandparents' dog had been dead for about a year.

Their experiences of the ghost continued soon after the party when my mother decided to re-paper my grandmother's bedroom and my grandmother, who was standing behind my mother, began to laugh all of a sudden. When my mum curiously asked her what it was that she was laughing at, my grandmother simply replied, 'You just glued my ghost to the wall.'

After redecorating my grandparents' house, my grandmother told my parents that there had been an increase in the number of disturbances. The television would cut on and off, the fan would go from high speed to off in a matter of seconds and doors would open and close when they stayed in the house.

My parents began to complain about feeling something crawling on their bed at night, and one night they were terrified by vicious growling they had heard behind their reclining chairs while they watched TV. It continued to happen so frequently that my stepfather would carry a gun if he was watching TV alone.

Being the realist I was, I looked for excuses and logical explanations, until my own experience led me to believe otherwise. One night I was in my room asleep and woke up to a slight tapping at my door. I must have said 'come in' at least 20 times, and when no one answered I fell back to sleep assuming that whatever the person wanted they no longer needed my assistance. About 10 minutes later I was woken up again by the same noise. I figured someone was trying to play a trick on me, so I slowly crept closer to the door, and when I heard the tapping I swung it open! No one was there. I walked cautiously out of my room expecting to catch someone down the hall, but there was no one there other than me.

I decided to use the bathroom before returning to my now very disturbed slumber. I began to feel uneasy, then a nervousness I had never experienced before swept over me as the bathroom lights flickered. I turned out the light, swung open the bathroom door and began slowly tiptoeing down the hallway towards my room.

I felt like I was being followed and I turned around to confirm my suspicion, and not an inch from my face stood a figure. It was not white or glowing but instead it was black and cold – so cold I could feel goose bumps on my skin. I turned and ran as fast as I could into my sister's room and leaped on top of her. I remember the two of us clinging to each other after I had explained what had happened. I guess that it was the ghost's way of proving itself, and that my logical explanations were way off.

CHEATING DEATH – DERBY

When I was 11 and in my first year of secondary school I had an encounter with the paranormal that left my friend and I seriously shaken.

I attended Bemrose Grammar School and the headmaster was Mr Eric Bennett, a man who did not suffer fools gladly and would be down on you like a ton of bricks should you run or misbehave in the school. There had always been stories of ghosts and strange sightings bandied about but nothing that we had ever believed, although the school did have an eerie feel to it.

One day a few friends and I were playing hide and seek in one of the buildings. I was with one of my friends and we were watching out for the others, getting ready to run if they came into sight. We were on the second floor near to a staircase and were peering between the banisters into the corridor beneath us.

I saw a large figure in what looked like a long black cloak come from one side of the corridor and move towards the other. It was really strange because there was no door on either the side it had come from or the side it headed towards. I just stared at it wondering who, or what, it was. It then turned its head and looked straight at me, but I could see no facial features due to its hood, except its eyes, which looked sunken into its face. Time seemed to stand still as it stared at me, and I could not move from fear. Suddenly it ran off and then disappeared as it walked through the wall.

I could not believe what I had seen and when I turned to my friend he was gazing in horror and disbelief. I casually asked if he had seen anyone, not wanting to hint that I had seen anything odd, when he started talking about a cloaked figure. He added that it had looked towards us with sunken eyes and I knew he had seen it too.

We ran, literally shaking, to find our friends and tell them about our paranormal encounter, but when we did they thought that we had fabricated the whole thing. However, they soon changed their minds when they saw how shaken we were. After calming down we joked that it may have been death himself and that we had cleverly outwitted him, but we never forgot the image of the figure which haunted our thoughts for the rest of our time at the school.

SOMEONE TO WATCH OVER ME – MICKLEOVER

My wife and I had recently moved into a new house on Ladybank Road in Mickleover. We were watching TV one night when I noticed she was staring at the wall slightly to the right of the set. I asked her what she was staring at and she was reluctant to answer me, but a few seconds later she admitted she could see a little girl about 10 years old standing next to the TV looking right at me. I thought nothing of it and presumed that my wife was over tired and imagining things.

One day my niece came to visit us. I was sitting on the settee drinking a can of beer and talking with my brother-in-law, when suddenly I noticed that my niece looked like she was scared or disturbed by something, so I asked her what was wrong. She said, 'I'm not lying about this, but I just saw a little girl about my age looking at me'.

I became curious and got up to investigate but could not see anything. I told her I could not see anything but that I also did not doubt what she was telling me because I had had two ghostly encounters in the past. She then told me to hold her hand because she was scared as the little girl was now walking by my side. She stayed there for about five minutes before, according to my niece, she disappeared. My wife told me a few weeks later that the little girl always watched me and that it was bugging her because she could not understand what was causing the apparition to have this attraction.

One night I finished work early as I was not feeling too well, and I came home at around 11am. I took a shower, got dressed and then went to fetch the wheelie bin as it had been emptied that morning. I took the rubbish outside to the bin, which was in front of the house by the street. I bent down to pick up another piece of rubbish I saw on the ground, and when I did so I had the strangest and most overwhelming feeling that someone was watching me from the front door of the house. I immediately looked at the door and saw no one was there, so I shook my head and said to myself 'that was weird'.

I immediately dismissed the feeling but I told my wife about it later that night, and she was convinced it was the little girl.

One month later I was making my lunch for work the next day at about 9pm. I finished making my sandwich and reached up to the cabinet to grab a sandwich bag, I turned my head a little bit towards my bedroom door, which was visible through the kitchen door, and out of the corner of my eye I finally saw the little girl. She was doing what she always did – watching me. I turned my head away initially because I had not realised exactly what I had seen and then turned my head back quickly when the truth finally dawned. She was gone.

I ran towards my bedroom and opened the door really fast. My wife was playing on the computer and nearly jumped out of her skin, and before I could say anything she cried 'I swear it felt like someone was standing outside that door right before you opened it!'

My wife had never told me what the little girl looked like, only that she was around 10 years old. When I described her as about 5ft tall, with blonde hair, skinny and wearing a white gown with green decorations on the bottom, which looked like stitch work from the late 1800s or early 1900s, to my amazement, she confirmed that what I had seen was exactly the same.

Well, from that day on I had no more encounters with her, but my wife saw her staring at me from time to time until we moved out.

STUDENT'S SURPRISE – DERBY

I started to experience strange things about five months ago, when I moved to Derby to start my university course.

I was lying on the sofa one night watching TV at around midnight when I looked in front of me at the reflection in the glass sliding doors and saw a pair of legs walk upstairs behind the sofa! I soon got used to the fact that there was something in the house and it did not bother me all that much. I could sometimes sense people standing right next to me in various parts of the house. One night I was watching TV and I heard a sound next to me as though someone had sat down, and I could see a big indent in the seat.

Another night, when I was getting ready for bed in my room, I looked up at the door way and could see a woman standing there in an old-fashioned dress. All of a sudden I got so hot that I thought I would faint. I grabbed my dressing gown and ran straight through her and out of the door to my room. I was terrified – sensing a presence was one thing, but this was just too much for me to cope with.

There was no way that I would return to my bedroom so I stood there semi-naked, banging on my flatmate's door. She took one look at my face and invited me straight in. After I explained what had happened we sat up all night not daring to go to sleep in case the ghost returned.

The following morning I went straight to a mystical shop in the Market Hall and asked the owner what I could do. She told me to 'smudge' the room with white sage, so I got some and burnt it in my room as soon as I got home. Thankfully I have not had any strange experiences since then and the ghost has left me to get on with my studies in peace.

FAMILIAR EYES - DOVEDALE

In 1996 my fiancée, two children and I lived in a small rented cottage near Dovedale in the Peak District National Park. The cottage's location was perfect for me as I had decided to quit the 'rat race' in order to find myself again after working in London as a banker for many years. I had been in a couple of circles that did Reiki and I used to fast in order to cleanse myself. We used to clean our cottage with smudge sticks, sounds and chanting.

Over the period of a couple of weeks I would wake up and there would be the face of a small child about eight years old stroking my face and looking right into my eyes. She had the classic green, misty silver light surrounding her and I could see her very clearly. I was not afraid of her; in fact, I felt very honoured that I was able to see her.

One night I meditated about what this child wanted me to do and I asked my spirit guides if I needed to perform a ceremony for her to send her back to the light, but I felt that was not what I needed to do. Then I wondered if she had a message for me, so I asked her out loud as I knew that she must have been listening.

One day I had gone to visit some friends in Manchester when I got a call on my mobile from my fiancée. She was frightened and crying, and as she was talking I could hear in the background what sounded like the cottage being smashed up. Suddenly there was a big crash, which sounded like the TV being thrown to the floor, and I knew I had to get home quickly.

I had to catch the train and when I got home the whole family was outside in the garden, clearly in a state of shock. My fiancée told me that she had called a spiritualist church minister about sending the ghost away, and when she hung up the phone strange and terrifying things started to happen, such as plates being violently smashed and books being thrown about. We believe that it was a psychic attack.

She called the minister again and he said he was on his way. I went into the cottage and found it was so cold, even though the central heating was on. I found my favourite book floating in the toilet and plates broken. The minister and his wife arrived and straight away they saw the child spirit in the cottage, still very angry, throwing what can only be described as a child's tantrum. They did their best to calm the spirit down and cleanse the cottage by saying prayers and dowsing the rooms with holy water.

After they had performed their rituals they asked if we had lost a child recently, and, stunned, we admitted that only a couple of months before my fiancée had suffered a miscarriage. On hearing this, the minister and his wife prayed with us.

A few months later I had a reading done by a medium and she told me that the spirit in the cottage was named Angelique and in another lifetime she and I had been brother and sister. I was the only person in her life to show her kindness and I had been sent away to fight in a war. When I did not return she ended her life and spent many years looking for her brother again. After searching for so long, when we tried to send her away she obviously did not want to go.

My fiancée and I married in 1997 and when I found out that my wife was pregnant I knew that she was going to have a baby girl. The second that she was born she opened her eyes and looked into mine for several seconds. I knew, somehow, that I had looked into those eyes before.

However, we did not name our new daughter Angelique – that might have been tempting fate a little too much.

THE MARCHING GHOST – UTTOXETER ROAD

One day I was on my way home from Bemrose School with my two friends, Rosie and Amy. We were running late one night after school, so we decided to take a shortcut through a graveyard on Uttoxeter Road, which led to Rosie's house.

We entered the graveyard and Rosie and Amy were posing for fun and messing around. Suddenly, I felt as though someone was watching me. Panicking, I ran away from my friends to try and get out of the graveyard, and they fell behind. I then climbed over the boundary wall and they followed soon after.

After I had regained my composure we re-entered the graveyard and started walking along a path which passed through the middle. All of a sudden, out of the corner of my eye, I saw something dressed all in white which appeared to be marching through the graveyard.

I froze and ignored it, and when I turned to see my friend she was also looking shaken. 'Did you see it?' I asked.

'The white person?'

'Yes.' I said, now completely unnerved. Whatever it was marched up and down again and then walked behind a tree but did not come out on the other side.

Feeling brave, we all went to investigate, but nobody was next to the tree. That did it. Terrified, we all had the feeling that eyes were all over our bodies and so we fled the graveyard screaming, with tears running down our faces.

Later that night, once we had calmed down, I was in Rosie's back garden and she was showing me the camera on her phone. Despite the fact that it was pitch black I took a picture of the garden, and when I looked at what I had photographed I was horrified to see a white head floating on its own against the black background. Totally in shock, I deleted the photograph as I felt that it would bring me bad luck.

Even today, whenever I have to walk past the cemetery on Uttoxeter Road I refuse to look inside for fear of seeing the marching ghost!

WEIRD FACE - OCKBROOK

My cousin and I were at a cemetery in Ockbrook with my grandmother because one of her friends had died, so we went to put flowers on her grave. My Gran was tending to the flowers and wanted some time alone at the grave, so my cousin and I decided to have a walk around.

At the back of the churchyard there was a little house, and as we approached it we saw this weird face, which appeared to be floating without a body above the ground. We both froze and stood there looking at it without saying anything to each other, and then I felt as if something was by my leg. I turned to look as it felt like a cat was rubbing up against me.

Boy was I wrong. Instead of seeing a cat I saw an old lady standing behind me, and she looked as though she was surrounded by a thin mist. I told myself that it was just my mind playing tricks on me after hearing about how haunted churchyards are. Then, just as I was thinking this, the lady disappeared into thin air right before my eyes.

My cousin screamed beside me. I asked if she was okay and she said that she heard something in her ear but wouldn't tell me what it was. We were both totally scared out of our wits.

We ran back to where our Gran was and told her everything, and she could tell from our faces that we were telling the truth. She simply told us to recite the Lord's Prayer! So we did, and as soon as we had finished we both felt immediately at peace.

THE ADVANCING EVIL - DERBY

My boyfriend and I decided to take a trip to Derby, as it is often described as the most haunted city in England, and while there we went on a ghost hunt.

As we do not come from the area, we did some research on the internet to find all the places that are supposed to be haunted, and on arrival we decided to go to Ye Olde Dolphin Inn as we had read that it is Derby's oldest alehouse.

The pub advertised the ghost hunt, lead by Richard Felix, so we took the tour, and were particularly interested in the underground tunnels that were mentioned. After the tour we chatted with the guide for a while, asking him more about the ghosts he had mentioned earlier and about any local cemeteries, as these have always been a source of interest to my boyfriend and I.

For some reason we took it upon ourselves to go and check out one of the cemeteries mentioned. Climbing the steep hill that led to the graveyard, we passed a line of trees. It was then that I noticed it was darker here than it had been on the tour, despite the fact that the tour had begun long after the sun had set – I could not understand it – the tour had been almost bright in comparison; the streets of Derby city had been warm and friendly. The walk up the hill was dark and cold, and the cemetery almost seemed to be screaming 'Go away!'

We continued on towards the graves, and my boyfriend noticed the change in atmosphere too. By the time we reached the cemetery my stomach was in knots and the hair on the back of my neck was standing straight up. I was gripping my boyfriend's hand so hard he had to pull away from me.

My boyfriend walked into the cemetery first. I followed, then suddenly I stopped in my tracks. I heard a quiet, high-pitched laughing. Though it was only barely audible, I could hear that it was so soft it was almost hoarse, yet was high-pitched and just unbearable. It was so awful – the most terrible sound I have ever heard.

I asked my boyfriend if he heard it but he hadn't. The laughter echoed in my head, as if it was daring me to keep looking around. I stopped walking at the edge of the cemetery, while my boyfriend was examining an old headstone. I called him back to where I was standing in a hushed, quick whisper as something evil was lurking. On the opposite side of the cemetery was another line of trees, and from within them I could feel a presence.

I could almost see the darkness spreading, and I could feel it moving towards us. My instincts told me that this was a place I should leave right away, so I called my boyfriend again, this time more frantically. When he came back to where I was standing I told him we needed to get out of there immediately.

A twig snapped in the distance, somewhere within the dark line of trees facing us and I froze. The darkness was creeping towards us, and a feeling of true malevolence spread to every inch of my body. I could literally see it getting darker and darker. I felt a giant, overwhelming presence looming before me. I had never felt anything like that. It was pure evil.

I then heard the hoarse, high-pitched laughter again, as if it was laughing at my fear. It started laughing because I could almost feel what it was feeling.

'What the hell was that?' my boyfriend whispered. I barely registered his voice in my entranced state. I was stuck, trapped, waiting for whatever it was to come and take me. Thankfully, I was snapped out of it when my boyfriend grabbed my hand, pulling me into a run. We ran down the hill, past the line of trees and back onto the well-lit streets.

'What the hell was that?' my boyfriend repeated after we caught our breath.

He told me that he had heard some evil sounding laughter. The hair on his neck and arms had been standing up and he knew that something was wrong. When he saw me standing there with a terrified look on my face, he knew it was time to get out of there.

LASER TAGGED - DERBY

My friends and I were all students and we decided to club together and buy a Laser Tag game so that we could have a laugh and kill time when we were not studying. We used to play in graveyards at night because the tombstones provided good cover and in the darkness it was easier to hide. I would like to point out, though, that we were always very respectful of the graves. Of course, the cemeteries we played in were scary places, but we were never really freaked out by this, although the setting did add a little fun to the game.

One night, four of us drove up to one of the cemeteries that we had played at several times before. Each previous visit had been uneventful. As we played and the night wore on eventually I wandered away and found myself alone towards the rear of the cemetery. It was not a large area, and about 10 minutes had passed since I had last seen anyone around.

I was about to go back up to where the car was, thinking perhaps everyone else was 'out' and I had just not heard them shout for a new game, when I saw movement about 20ft away, behind one of the gravestones. I ducked down so that the stone in front of me gave me some cover and I watched.

Right before my eyes, a dark silhouette rose as if it had been in hiding in back of the stone. It was in the shape of a person, slightly hunched over, but even as close as I was I could not distinguish any of its features.

The shadow moved quickly from the stone to another one about 5ft away and hunched down again. Convinced that I had spotted one of my pals, perhaps one of the guys on the other team, I slowly crept forward to jumping out and shoot him with my laser pistol.

I never took my eyes off of the stone as I crept up slowly, and when I got close I sprang forward to get in a shot. To my horror, there was no one there, and the hair rose on the back of my neck as I realised I had actually seen a ghost. My fears were confirmed when I ran back up to the car and saw the other three players standing next to it having a smoke.

When I explained what I had seen they joked about it, saying I was seeing things, but I have never forgotten it and have no idea who or what it was.

We started playing paintball after that, which did not involve cemeteries at night, and that was just fine by me!

GHOST GIRL - DERBY

When I was in my second year as a student at Derby University I rented a room in a shared house just off Burton Road. I was on my way home from a friend's house one night and, just for fun, decided to walk home through the cemetery as I had never walked that way before. However, when I entered I felt really scared because I believe in ghosts, and although I wanted to see one I knew that if I did I would be petrified.

Just as I was about to walk through the gates of the cemetery, I saw a girl a few feet away. I walked over and asked her, 'Aren't you afraid to walk through the cemetery at night?'

She replied, 'I was when I was alive. But now I'm not.'

I turned to ask her what she meant but she had disappeared. I felt a chill pass over me and I turned on my heels and ran as fast as I could out of the cemetery gates and all the way back to my house.

I told my housemates what had happened but they did not believe me. However, in all my time in Derby if ever I suggested we walked through the cemetery they always made up excuses and walked another way.

NOT GOING BACK - KINGSWAY

I needed to go to the Sainsbury's at Kingsway, and as I did not have any petrol and as it was a nice day I decided that I would walk the short distance from my home on Manor Road past Kingsway Hospital.

On the way there I saw an old man. He looked at me and waved. The next day I was riding my mini-motorcycle and saw the same old man in the same clothes that he was wearing the first time I saw him.

I mentioned him to my friend Charley but she didn't see anything odd about it. Our conversation quickly turned to the subject of ghosts and how haunted Kingsway must be. She just said, 'I don't believe in ghosts.' So I dared her to walk past Kingsway Hospital at midnight on the coming Friday, which was Friday the 13th.

She said she would, but as the day dawned I felt guilty and told her she did not have to go, but if she did I was going to give her £20. I went home to bed but could not sleep. I kept thinking about the old man and about Charley out by herself, so I decided to go and find her.

I checked my watch and it was 11.45pm. I tried phoning Charley but there was no answer so I guessed that she was on her way to Kingsway and decided that I should walk there too to make sure that she was okay.

To my surprise, as I approached Kingsway I saw the old man again. This time I stopped to see if he would chat with me. He approached me and said, 'If you are looking for your friend, check the tree behind me.'

So, hoping to give my friend a bit of a fright, I crept to the tree and yelled, 'BOO!' Charley jumped from behind the tree.

She said, 'Why were you talking to yourself a minute ago?'

I replied, 'I was talking to an old man, he told me where you were hiding.' I felt a chill run down my spine as she explained that there had been no one next to me and she had only hidden behind the tree when she saw me coming down the road. She told me there was nobody else around and she had not spoken to anyone.

I have never seen the old man since, but, my encounter was enough to make Charley believe in ghosts!

WAIT FOR ME! – BUXTON

My family bought a house in north Derbyshire, just outside Buxton. One day, when I was 14, I was on my way home from school and decided to take a shortcut through the churchyard as I was feeling cold and there was something that I wanted to watch on the television when I got in.

The churchyard was quiet as no one was about, but when I was about halfway through the cemetery I heard a voice call, 'Wait! Wait for me!' It was the strangest sound that I had ever heard, as it did not quite sound human but it was not an animal noise either.

The voice totally freaked me out and I did not have the guts to look back because I was too scared. I ran as fast as I could and had almost reached the gate when I heard the voice again. This time, plucking up all my courage, I turned to see where the voice was coming from, but all I could see was a white mist swirling from the ground. Frightened at what I had just witnessed, I ran all the way home.

When I got home I told my mum about my experience in the graveyard and she took me back to the churchyard gate. We looked on the ground but did not see anything out of place and there was no sign of the strange, swirling mist. However, I know that what I saw and heard was real.

WHO HANDED OVER THAT TOOL? – BREADSALL

About three or four years ago my brother Andrew and I were really bored because it was the last Saturday of the summer holidays, all our friends seemed to be away and there was nothing to do in Breadsall. I asked him if he wanted to go to the fields to make a den.

Glad to finally be doing something, we walked through the fields behind our house for about six minutes until we got to a huge tree near a church. We had found the perfect place for us to build a den. Andrew put the tools and other things next to the tree. I started building and yelled at him over my shoulder, 'Bring me a tool!' But there was no answer. Eventually he passed me a tool. 'Thank you, Andrew.' I said.

'What?' He asked, puzzled. He was over the other side of the tree, several metres away!

I looked up and gasped, 'Andrew, did you just give me a tool?'

'No,' he replied, 'I was over here picking this wood up. Why?'

I felt myself go really hot as fear and realisation sank in. A ghostly boy had given me the tool to help me build the den!

I ran and ran, and I never stopped until I arrived at our house. I was crying and panting. Andrew followed behind me not knowing why I was running or looking so scared.

I whispered, 'I think I saw a ghost in the field and he just gave me a tool! I thought it was you.' We were both so scared that we never returned to the field or our den, and it was the first time that we could not wait to get back to school.

THE MAN WITH NO EYES – DALE ABBEY

I was in Dale Abbey last year with some of my friends. We were walking through the ruins, talking, when I saw a man in a dark robe walking towards the arch.

None of my friends had seen him, and after I told them which direction he had walked in we started searching for him. We spotted him standing underneath the archway and shouted to him to get his attention, at which he turned around.

The memory of what happened next will stay with us all forever because as soon as we shouted out the man started to float towards us, about 6ft above the ground. We tried to run but seemed to be rooted to the spot by fear. Suddenly he passed behind me and I felt my legs again, so I started to run. When I turned to look again the figure took his hood off his head and I saw that he had no eyes, just a void where his head should have been.

We ran all the way to the local pub and spoke to an old regular there, who told us that we had probably seen the ghost of a monk.

1842 – LANGLEY MILL

People say pets sense ghosts more easily than humans. Well, that is certainly true when it comes to my three cats, who made me aware of the ghost that is haunting us – the ghost of a little Victorian girl called Catherine.

I live in an old house in Langley Mill, just outside Heanor. One night I was in bed with my partner, but I couldn't sleep because my cats kept growling at the foot of the bed. I switched the camera on my phone on to create some light so I didn't have to get up, and I saw a little girl standing there, smiling at me, just visible in the semi-darkness.

I was so scared, but I did not move from the bed. She said she meant no harm but was looking for her mother, so I explained that her mother was not here and that maybe she is in the light. Then she told me her name was Catherine and asked me what year it was. I told her it was 2008, and she said it was 1842!

Since that night my partner and I have got used to her being around. She plays with my cats by throwing the toys about and opening the bedroom door for them, and I have no intention of bringing anyone in to get rid of her as she is causing no harm to anyone. In fact, in a way my partner and I find it comforting to know that we have someone watching over us.

FOUR HEADS - DERBY

When my cousin Sarah was eight she never liked to be left alone in her room. One day I asked her why, and she replied, 'Jodie, there's four men's heads floating, and I'm really scared.'

Unsure what to make of this revelation, I told her mum and she immediately got an old photograph out. She showed it to Sarah, who picked out three of the faces in the picture as the same as those she had seen in her bedroom. The scary thing was, everybody on that photograph had been dead for a long time. They were the faces her grandfathers and great uncles, whom she had never met as they lived in London when they were alive.

Since the identity of three of the faces were discovered, Sarah has never seen them again.

THE CELLAR GHOST - DERBY

A little while ago my friends decided they wanted to have a séance in my cellar. I let them do it, but I did not want to be part of it. They decided to use a Ouija board to add a little bit more 'scariness'. They wanted to call upon my friend's deceased mother.

On the day of the séance everything was set: my friends and I were all in my cellar and so it began. My friend, who had been elected spokesperson, kept messing around and said a different name – Shelby Quinn. All of a sudden we heard tapping noises, and fear started to set in. My friend then said, 'Show us another couple of signs that you are here.' The taps turned on and off, the lights started to flicker all over the house and our candles went out. The bathroom door started to open and close quietly; then it slammed shut and opened fast, this time breaking the door. Then, to our horror, we heard loud screaming that sounded like a young lady.

Ever since the séance strange things have been happening. Every now and then pictures will move, and sometimes the ghost that we evoked will make a mess of my cellar. Once my friend and I even saw her: she had messy black hair, wore a blue wedding dress with bloodstains on it and had a knife in her hand.

HOW DID HE KNOW? - DERBY

I have a younger cousin who is about three and is always having strange experiences.

One night he was in bed and his mum was downstairs, and she heard his toys shaking on the monitor. She went to check on him then went back downstairs. After a few minutes she heard the same thing once more and she checked him again and told him to go back to sleep.

The next morning she asked him why he would not go to sleep, and he replied, 'Mummy, that man with the light on his hat was playing with my toys.' My aunt thought this was strange, and she was then amazed and shocked to find out that the house was built on land that used to be part of a coal pit.

Later that week, my young cousin was in his room by himself. He was talking to himself, saying, 'I won't tell Mummy. I promise.'

His mum ran upstairs in shock and asked him what was going on, and he replied, 'Mummy, that strange man is asking me to go out the window with him, but I don't want to.'

Shocked by what my cousin had said, that night my aunt decided to let him sleep in her bed. As she lay there she felt an enormous weight on her, pinning her to the bed. The phenomenon happened once to my aunt and also to her husband, after which they had the house exorcised. Nothing has happened since and my cousin has never spoken about the 'man with the light on his hat' again.

ANGEL FRIEND - ALVASTON

As a child growing up in Alvaston I used to talk to a blonde-haired spirit girl who would appear in the corner of my bedroom. She was the most beautiful girl I had ever seen and had a golden ring around her head. I learnt very early on that nobody else could see her and so I kept it to myself.

My mum has always been very spiritual and reads tarot cards, but even she could not see my friend. She wanted to use her gift full-time and decided to do readings for people on a psychic phone line. After only a few weeks of doing this she made friends with another psychic. One day, her psychic friend asked, 'Did you know that your daughter used to talk to angels? One day they came to her when she was around seven years old. They told her very important things.'

I wish now that I could remember what they said, but maybe subconsciously I do. Thank you, angels, for watching over me and guiding me to the Light.

THE GHOST OF THE ATTIC – DERBY

One night I was lying in bed in my room, which was a converted attic, when I heard a sudden bang. I shot up out of bed to see what it was, but on investigating I heard nothing except the sound of rain beating on my window. I went back to sleep but kept hearing those sounds thumping through my head all night and for months afterwards.

A few days later I was sitting with my dad and sisters and he was trying to scare us by telling us stories about a green ghost that lives in our attic. Of course, I did not believe him, and he went on to say that at midnight every night the ghost appears and knocks at the window of my room! My dad sent me to bed at midnight to prove his point, but I still did not believe him as he is known for being a practical joker.

I went to bed just after midnight and then my attic door flung open despite the fact that it was bolted shut. I flew down the stairs to find my dad innocently sitting on the sofa. He just turned to me and said, 'Did you hear it? It's freaky, isn't it?'

I agreed and tentatively went back up to bed. As I lay there, still a little shaken, I heard tapping at my window. I slowly crept out of bed and flung open my curtains, and right there in front of the glass I saw a mysterious cloud of green fog. I was so scared, but finding some courage from somewhere I told it to go away and asked why it was here. I left my room and I decided to stay in my sister's room that night!

ANGRY SPIRIT – UTTOXETER ROAD

I used to live in a block of flats not far away from the cemetery on Uttoxeter Road. When my brother and I were teenagers we invited several of our friends over to the flat to play a game of dare, which culminated (as it often did) with the challenge of having to run through the cemetery.

It was such a rush to be in the cemetery at night. On this occasion, however, my brother and his friends decided to hang out, smoke cigarettes and drink beer instead.

As I waited with a couple of my friends at the other side we could hear yelling and shouting coming from the darkness. It was my brother and his two friends, who suddenly came running out of the cemetery. Shaking, they told us they had been sitting in front of a small crypt when they heard a loud, eerie hissing sound behind them.

They turned to see what it was and saw what looked like a spirit standing behind them. As they started to run the ghostly figure floated after them. It disappeared after it chased them out of the cemetery and my brother swore that he would never go into the cemetery at night again.

COMPUTER FACE – STENSON

A little while ago I was staying at my mum's house in Stenson for a few days, and one night I had a friend over to stay. She and I were having a great time on the computer, talking to our friends and taking photographs of the house to try and use up all of the film in my camera.

I told her to take a photograph of our friends' faces that were on the computer screen. Later we had the film developed and took the prints back to my mum's house to have a good look at them.

We were flicking though the photographs, which to be honest were fairly unremarkable, when suddenly we were stopped in our tracks and nearly dropped the prints in shock. There, on one of the photos of our friends on the computer screen, was a face, not one of our friends' but a weird face. It looked as if it had its 'hand' resting under it.

We didn't know what it was for a long time, until we found out that an old man had died in the house some time ago. Could we have captured his spirit on our photograph? My mum told me that she had always thought there was something in the house, because things would go missing and then turn up again where she had already looked.

So many strange things happened in the house, but we had never captured an image on a photograph before, nor have we had any luck since.

LAUGHING DEMON – OAKWOOD

In the winter of 1995 I had just divorced my husband and was renting a small house in Oakwood. I chose the house because I have always had a fear of old houses and this one was new, and as it was the first time I had been on my own since I was young I decided that I needed to feel safe in my own home.

The house was a very nice detached house, but it had no storage apart from an understairs cupboard, and, for some strange reason, every time I went near it a strange sense of dread filled my entire body. So, to avoid the feeling, I decided that I would not use it.

One day I was vacuuming the hallway when I heard a strange sound whch I thought was laughter coming from inside the cupboard. It sounded sinister like the laugh you hear from cartoon villains. I decided I needed to be brave and finally took a look in the cupboard. However, as soon as I opened the door a rush of cold air seemed to fly at me and I started to feel faint.

All of a sudden, the laugher stopped, but then just as I began to blame my overactive imagination, the sinister laughter started again, this time in the lounge, and it got louder and louder. As I have said before, the house was detached so it could not be coming from a neighbour's house, so my first thought was that maybe there was someone outside laughing and I went to investigate. I opened the front door but nobody was around so I returned to the lounge, where the laughing continued.

I was terrified initially, but suddenly I felt this almighty courage in me and I shouted at the laughter, 'You have no place here, go back to where you came from!' As soon as I had done so the room went really bright and the air went very cold again before it fell silent.

I fell, exhausted and confused, onto the sofa, and while I caught my breath I noticed that all the houseplants in the room had all drooped and their leaves had turned brown.

To this day I do not know what the laughing was all about, and I moved out of that house as soon as possible.

THE SLEEPOVER - OCKBROOK

My family lived in our home in Ockbrook for 15 years. Believe it or not, we shared the house with a deceased woman who did not realise she was dead. Numerous strange things occurred throughout the years, and my family became so used to her being there they nicknamed the poor soul Maggie.

One night my uncle had to spend the night with us as his own house had been flooded in Shardlow. He woke up in the night as the blankets were pulled off his bed and dresser drawers violently opened and shut. I had never heard a grown man scream before!

That was his last sleepover; he slept in the car the following night out on our driveway!

ASKING FOR HELP? – DERBY

I was studying media studies at college and as part of some coursework I had to write an article for a magazine. Well, being into the paranormal I decided that I would write on the subject and so I started interviewing people about their experiences. My tutor said that I could interview her to help me with the project and we arranged a meeting, but she refused to meet me in the classroom, preferring the canteen.

When I began the interview, my tutor said that she had had some strange experiences when in the college alone. One experience occurred when she had been alone in a particular part of the college, packing up her books. She heard a noise like someone was fixing books in the library next door, but she thought nothing of it because she assumed another tutor was in there doing research.

But, as she had listened, the noise changed. She heard cabinets opening and closing and noises like animals fighting each other. She quickly went into the room to confront whoever it was, but no one was there, and she was confronted with the incredible sight of books flying around on their own.

She told me she had run like a mad woman to the road and never looked back, terrified in case she saw something. That was the end of the interview.

Personally, I think that the ghost was just making its presence known and just wanted to let her know that it needed help with something. Whatever its reasons, after that incident my tutor never wanted to be alone in college again.

NOT SO FUN FACTORY – DERBY

A few years ago, when I was 16, I used to work in a Fun Factory in Derby. Every night at 9pm I would tidy up the play area in return for free ice cream.

I did the job for over a year and loved it, until the night when a strange incident occurred. I was tidying up the balls from the ball pool, as usual, when suddenly, from the corner of my eye, I noticed a little girl crying and covering her face with her hands. I walked over to where she was sitting, on the bottom of the red slide which led into the ball pool. She was dressed quite nicely, had lovely blonde hair, and I guessed that she was about five years old.

As I approached her I asked if she was okay, but she never moved or stopped crying. I asked again, louder this time in case she had not heard me, but still nothing. I walked right up to her and went to put my arm around her, but as I did so she disappeared before my eyes.

Because I was young myself, you can imagine how scared I was, and I ran all the way back home to my dad in floods of tears. I was so shaken by what I saw that I never went back there again.

THE GIRL BY THE ROAD - DERBY

I do not, as a rule, pick up hitchhikers, especially in this day and age, but back in the 1960s it did not seem such a big deal as I think we trusted people more. And that was certainly my mindset, until one night when I experienced the following after picking up a stranger on the road...

I had worked the second shift at Rolls-Royce for about 20 years and usually stayed until 6am a few times a week. One night as I was driving home I saw a young girl walking by the road. It was very early in the morning and pouring down with rain, so I thought I should pull over and offer her a lift.

She was very pretty, with long blonde hair and a smile that was hypnotising. She got in and told me where she lived, so we made our way there. As I drove she was very quiet and never took her eyes off the road. I could not help but notice her perfume, as I had never smelt anything like it in my life, and nor have I since.

Eventually, we arrived at her house, and to my surprise I saw that it was a run down old condemned place that looked like it had not been occupied for some time. Puzzled, I asked her if she was sure this was her place. She said yes, thanked me for the ride and got out without another word.

As I drove away feeling a little uneasy about the whole episode, I looked back at her one more time, and I almost swallowed my tongue in horror. When I looked back, instead of seeing my beautiful passenger I saw what looked like a large man with hoofed feet and a long tail that came to a point. There was no sign of the girl, only the strange, demonic figure. From that day forward I never picked up a hitchhiker again.

'YOU'RE RUINING MY LIFE!' - DERBY

My family and I lived in a house that was over 100 years old, but despite the age of the house I never once thought it would be haunted. However, when I was 14, I was faced with the terrible realisation that there was, in fact, a ghost in the house – and that is when everything began to go wrong.

I was having a great year. I was doing well at school, I had loads of friends and everything was going smoothly at home. Halloween was approaching and I decided to throw a party and invite all my friends, and I thought that it would be the perfect chance to impress a guy I fancied!

In our lounge we had a large china cabinet, which had two locked doors at the front that required a key to open. I decided that the cabinet would look perfect if it was decorated with some orange and black streamers, to add to the Halloween mood, so I ran upstairs to find the streamers and all of a sudden I heard a loud CRASH.

I flew downstairs towards the noise, which sounded like it had come from the lounge. When I entered, to my horror I saw that the doors to the china cabinet were somehow unlocked and the whole top row of plates had been thrown onto the ground. A little scared, I mused over how it could have happened as I was the only one home. Dismissing the event as just one of those things, I grabbed the brush and swept up the mess, and then I continued to decorate the house.

Ding dong! The first guest arrived and everything was set up perfectly. I had awesome music playing, black lights that made everything glow and lots of creepy decorations. One by one, my friends started piling in.

In the middle of the party, however, strange things started to happen. We were having a great time, and the music was so loud you had to shout, but then, despite the noise from the stereo, we all suddenly heard loud, thunderous footsteps coming from the floor above us. I rolled my eyes, thinking it might have been my little brother David trying to scare us.

I ran upstairs to tell David to stop, but halfway there I realised that my brother was at his friend's house. I froze. Who else could it be? My mum was in the kitchen and my dad had left us when I was a small child. My heart raced. I mustered up enough courage to finish walking up the stairs, but when I got to the landing there was nothing to be seen. By now more than a little shaken, I went back downstairs, trying to stop myself thinking about it.

It was getting late, so we all decided to sit around the TV in the dark and watch a scary movie. When everyone was sitting around in an excited huddle, I went to turn off the lights. I sat back down in front of the TV, trying to engineer it so that I was next to Josh, the boy I liked, but just as the film started the lights flickered back on. Annoyed, I got up to go shut them off, but I could see that the switch was still flicked to the OFF setting. My eyes were wide as I stumbled back to my seat but then the lights went off again.

A little while into the film Josh went upstairs. He had been gone for a couple of minutes when suddenly we heard sounds like somebody falling down the stairs. We all ran out of the lounge and saw Josh lying at the bottom of the stairs obviously in pain. He stared up at us and told us that he had been pushed.

Someone looked accusingly at me and said, 'What did you do to him?'

'What?' I cried. 'I was sitting on the sofa the whole time!' Things were starting to get far too scary.

After a few minutes of nervous chatter, Josh's parents came and picked him up. The rest of us sat back down on the sofa and continued watching the movie. All of a sudden, the TV set flickered and blacked out. The room then got VERY cold, and I could see my own breath misting in the darkness.

We all just sat there, shaken, then suddenly we heard a scream from upstairs. Terrified, I turned the lights on and dashed upstairs, and everyone followed me. I crept nervously towards where I thought the scream had come from – my mum's bedroom. I opened the door, dreading what I might see, but all I saw was my mum reading. I asked her what on earth she was screaming about and she just looked at me like I was insane. I could tell my guests were scared out of their minds by now, and many of them had started to call their parents.

Once the house was empty, I went to my room and cried. The night had been a horrible, scary failure. As I lay there sobbing, I heard a soft willowy voice call my name. It said 'Jessica, now we can be together...alone.' It was a man's voice.

The room went freezing cold, just as it had downstairs. I was now totally convinced that I was being haunted; the voice, the sudden drop in temperature, things breaking and the lights failing. I hid under my covers and somehow managed to fall asleep.

At school the next day everyone avoided me in the hallway; no one even dared to make eye contact with me. This treatment continued and I fell into a deep state of depression. My grades started going down and pretty soon I was failing at school.

A few weeks later, when I was going to sleep, I heard the ghostly voice again and the room was once more like Antarctica. I was sick and tired of this. 'Go away!' I screamed at the top of my lungs. 'I hate you!' I was sobbing now. 'You're ruining my life!'

I picked up my glass piggy bank and, furious and desperate, threw it at the wall. It smashed into tiny pieces. Suddenly the voice stopped, and I no longer felt as though there was anyone, or anything, there. The room began to warm, and I cried myself to sleep.

Since that final encounter everything has been nice and quiet. Once in a while a cupboard opens by itself, but I am okay with that. Eventually I convinced some of my friends to come over and I think I was as relieved as they were that nothing happened. Soon I earned everyone's trust back and things started going well for me once more.

RED EYES IN THE AIR - CHATSWORTH

A friend and I were both leaders at Peak 85, which was a scouting camp held at Chatsworth in Derbyshire. It was a massive event with scout and guide troops coming from all over the world to join together and have fun.

One afternoon I was talking with my friend, and as the afternoon became evening our conversation turned to the subject of religion. We were having a great time talking and discussing our faith in the evening glow. Eventually the sun set and it became dark enough that it was difficult to see one another, but we still lingered outside the tents. We were sitting in a fenced-in area between two tents, and to my right was a small gravel road, then a wood line and the entire field of tents beyond.

As we chatted, I became aware that something was moving in a small wood to my left, but the sound was distant and soft so I didn't really give it any thought. As we continued with our conversation, however, the sound of something walking became noticeable and then I heard a soft exhale. It seemed to be closer to us that before, but whatever it was it was still masked by the darkness of the wood. I stopped listening to my friend and focused on the strange noise, and he noticed I was distracted. Then, to my amazement, he asked if I had heard the noise as well. We both described the same noise coming from the wood, which then became louder and louder as if it was approaching us. I could make out the gravel road in the moonlight, and the wood line, but the forest was too dark to see into.

We stood up, by now completely puzzled and all the while the noise grew louder; the exhaling became so very loud.

Then, right there in the darkness, we saw something that neither of us will ever forget. About six or seven feet up in the air there were two red eyes – two red, glowing, burning, blazing eyes – staring at us. We slowly walked backwards away from the eyes towards the tent, scared out of our wits.

As I reached the door of the tent I heard it on the gravel, running after us. We gasped for breath, scared to death, and I was in tears as we dived inside. My friend grabbed his flashlight and said he was going back out.

As he slowly opened the zip we could still hear it, but as he lit up the area with his light there was nothing to be seen.

No human could have left the area without a trace so fast, and no animal, to my knowledge or experience, behaves or looks like that. I have never forgotten that night nor the fear I felt. It haunts my thoughts, and I fear seeing those terrible eyes again.

MORNING EVIL - WILLINGTON

I lived alone in Willington in my first house. I had worked hard to buy it and had only been living there for a week when I had my first ghostly encounter.

It all started at 3.00am sharp when I was watching Sky TV in the living room. I heard laughter coming from the kitchen, but dismissed it at first as I thought it was just me.

At about 3.15am I heard a sudden crash from the kitchen, and this time I ran over to investigate, although I was still not scared at this point. Two of my dishes had fallen and were broken. I cleaned up the mess and thought that it was probably mice or something. Just then, as I walked out, I felt something rub on my shoulder as though someone was trying to get my attention, and then I felt scared.

I turned around, not knowing what to expect, and suddenly I felt the temperature drop and heard laughing once more. I fled up the stairs, afraid I had an intruder, and came down with my baseball bat. I saw no one, but as I looked at the kitchen window I saw, there in the glass, a man with horns. It was like a drawing in fog.

I screamed, ran outside as fast as I could and stayed out there for several minutes. When I eventually ventured back inside and plucked up the courage to look in the window once more, the face was gone and the temperature was back to normal. I was so shaken up I could not sleep for three days.

THE NIGHT VISITOR - DERBY

I worked the night shift at a nursing home in Derby for a number of years, and on my first shift at the home my fellow employees decided to tell me that the place was haunted. I did not believe them, of course, and dismissed their claims as a wind-up that was probably played on all new employees. How wrong I was.

One night some time later, while I was in an old gentleman's room doing the usual night-time rounds, I heard something that sounded like the shuffling of feet coming from the far side of the room. I turned and glanced at the bed but the old gentleman was sound asleep. There was a pause, and then I heard the noise again.

When I turned in the direction of the sound, my eye caught something in the mirror. I peered closer and saw the image of a little boy. I just stood there looking at him, frozen, and he looked back at me. Suddenly he spoke to me, saying, 'Please let my grandfather out of here so we can go home.'

I left that room as fast as I could, too shocked to tell my colleagues what I had seen. A few days later the old man passed away, and I hope that his grandson, if that was indeed who I saw, came to take him into the next life. I never again doubted that the home was haunted!

Evil eyes - Derby

About a year ago I was standing outside my friend's house in the centre of Derby, and I had the most terrifying experience of my life.

My friend's sister, Nadine, was a Goth and was into witchcraft and all things spiritual. She had recently bought a book called *The Necronomicon* and it had a whole bunch of symbols in it for gates and demons, and even the devil. Nadine loved the book so much that she wrote all of the symbols on the walls in her old bedroom, including the bad ones.

Anyway, on the night in question, I was at their house, standing outside and waiting for my friend to grab her stuff, when something caught my eye in one of the upstairs windows. It was Nadine's bedroom. I stepped closer to the house and peered forwards to get a better look and I saw two glowing red eyes staring right at me. Whatever it was looked at me, grinned and turned away. I was so scared that I ducked down and hid behind my friend's dad's car. Eventually she came out, but I was so shaken I could not speak. I never told her what I saw in her sister's window, and I never will.

Reaching for Howard - Willington

When I was younger, during the summer holidays I often spent the day with my friend Jessica as both my parents were out at work My mum dropped me off at Jessica's house in Willington, as usual, and I was surprised to find that my friend had been given a kitten by her parents as a present. It was the cutest thing I had ever seen and my friend named him Howard, after her favourite member of Take That.

During the day we took Howard up to her room and played with some balls and cotton reels with him, but the little kitten disappeared under Jessica's bed and did not come out for a while.

Thinking that he may have been trapped, I lay on the floor and took a peek under the bed. There, just a few inches away, was Howard, and he was frozen with fear. I soon understood why – looking straight at me, lying by Howard under the bed, was the ghost of an old lady. I screamed as loud as I could! Jessica, frightened by my scream, also looked under the bed to see what was the matter. Upon seeing the old lady she grabbed Howard, screamed like I was and we both ran downstairs to tell her mum.

WHITE DRESS WOMAN - HATTON

I was going on a trip to Derby to visit my cousins, and while I was on the bus I looked out the window to see the view of Hatton.

There, not too far distant, I could see what looked like a woman dressed entirely in white. I rubbed my eyes to see if I was imagining her, but when I looked again she was still there. For a spilt second I thought I saw green eyes, then the bus passed her and my view was blocked. Despite the fact that my view of her was brief I was so scared.

However, the return journey was even more scary. As the bus passed the same spot later that day I saw her again, but this time she was closer, and she seemed to have a silver hue about her. Because I was so intrigued, and also possibly because I wanted a logical explanation for what I had seen, I decided that I would get off at the next stop and go and have a look for her. I made my way back to where I thought the white lady was standing, and as I approached I could just make out her figure, still standing there in her silvery-white dress. As I got close to her, she vanished, and I have never run so quick in my life. Now when I am on the bus and pass that spot I never dare to look out of the window.

THE INJURED GIRL - SPONDON

One night I was babysitting my little sister at my parents' house in Spondon. It was getting very late and my parents were due home anytime soon. Not that it mattered, however, as I had not heard a peep out of my little sister all night, which was rather disappointing as I love her to bits. I actually used to like it when she could not sleep as it meant we got more time together.

Just before midnight I got up to go to the toilet upstairs, when suddenly I heard someone running downstairs really fast, then I heard a big thump and a scream. Thinking it was my little sister, I ran to the stairs, but when I got to there, instead of seeing my little sister I saw a different little girl at the bottom of the steps. I was horrified to see that her legs and arms were twisted at odd angles, and she was crying and screaming. Then she disappeared, right before my eyes. I ran to my sister's room to check if she had heard anything, but she was fast asleep.

I couldn't wait for my parents to get home, and after that night I never went upstairs by myself again!

THINGS THAT GO BUMP IN THE NIGHT – DERBY

I am 15 and have lived in Derby all my life. One night a little while ago I was home alone and I was dreading going to bed because I always had dreams of strange creatures under my bed and a feeling that something evil lurked there. I know it sounds crazy but that is how I felt, and I just could not shake the feeling. I even used to wait until midnight to go to bed so that I would be that tired I would drop off immediately.

That particular night I went to bed at midnight as normal, and I was just drifting off to sleep when I heard the most horrifying, bloodcurdling scream come from under my bed.

I sprang awake, with my heart beating out of my chest and I looked under my bed – my eyes were wide with horror. There, lying beneath me, was the ghost of a woman and a small black object next to her. I screamed and ran downstairs to wait for my parents.

Ever since that night I have been able to see her under my bed, but no one else can and I know what I see is real even if my family think I am just imagining it.

WEBCAM GHOST – HEANOR

I never believed in ghosts, or anything paranormal for that matter, until I had a ghostly experience in 2007. In fact, had my entire family not witnessed the encounter at the same time I don't think I would have believed my eyes.

It started off just like any other evening in my house in Heanor, where I lived with my husband and my nine children. That night everyone in the house was busy doing their own thing and my husband and I were watching TV downstairs with our youngest children, when all of a sudden my son Kevin screamed from his bedroom, and it did not sound like a 'play fight' type of scream. With nine children in the house, my husband and I were used to screams and shouting coming from upstairs, but this scream was different. Both my husband and I dashed to our feet and ran up the stairs to see what the problem was.

As we approached Kevin's room we saw that the other children had congregated near the entrance to his bedroom door as they too wanted to know why he was screaming. We opened the door and went inside to find him sat at his computer with his mouth wide open.

'Look at this mum!' He said, pointing at the computer screen. There on the screen was a girl he had been talking to over the webcam and behind her was what looked like the ghost of a woman, and it appeared to be floating in and out of the room.

Amazed, and still not sure whether I believed my eyes or not, I called my husband over and we all stood there totally gobsmacked as my son typed a warning to his friend.

He typed, and as soon as she received the message she turned round to have a look.

'THERE IS NOTHING THERE. YOU DAFT SOD' was her reply.

No matter how many times he told her that there was a ghost, she simply did not believe him, so I introduced myself and assured her that there was. At this the girl shot up out of the room and went to find her mum.

As we looked at the screen we could see the ghost floating across the girl's room and through the walls, then it floated into the middle of the room, stopped and turned to look at the computer. We were all screaming and could not believe what we were seeing.

To our horror the ghost then floated forward and looked right at the webcam, giving us a full view of her. She had long scraggy grey hair and black eyes and her hands and face looked as though she had been burnt. My son managed to take some still photographs of her with the webcam while it was looking straight at us.

Then suddenly it floated back and seemed to be hovering on the chair as my son's friend came back into the room and immediately went to sit in the chair.

'DON'T SIT DOWN...IT'S ON YOUR CHAIR' he typed, but again she did not believe him and sat right down on it!

We could see on the screen that the ghost was now stroking her hair, and at this point my son's friend started to feel cold and scared. Suddenly, the ghost floated up in the air and through the wall and we never saw it again – but we were all left gobsmacked.

A few days later my son found out that part of the old farmhouse that his friend lived in had been destroyed by fire many years ago and had to be rebuilt. Could it have been the ghost of someone who perished in the fire?

We kept the photographs taken by my son for a while, but to be honest they frightened me so much that I had to burn them. Needless to say, I am a sceptic no longer.

THE MAN ON TV - ETWALL

I have had paranormal experiences since I was a child. I have talked to my mother about the subject and our family just seems predisposed to it. The following incident is the first I can really remember, other than vague impressions from when I was a toddler. I had experienced feelings of being watched many times in my house but nothing had ever happened before.

I was 16 years old and had saved up my babysitting and pocket money to buy my first TV; a black and white with silver casing. One night I was getting ready for bed and experienced the familiar feeling that I was being watched. I decided to ignore it as it usually passed, so I put my nightclothes on, turned off the TV and got into bed. I was about to turn off the light, when something on the TV screen caught my eye. I stopped to look what it was and became rooted to the spot in horror.

There, on the black screen, was the back of a man's head, with long, brown hair. The head slowly turned towards me and I saw a moustache and light goatee beard. The face was very angry, and it looked really thin and tense. It turned all the way to face me, stared directly at me for a moment and then screamed! There was no sound at all, but I could feel its anger.

I ran out of my room to where my parents were sitting, oblivious to the terrifying events unfolding in my bedroom. They questioned me but I told them I was getting some water as I was too afraid to say anything to them. My mind raced as I tried to decide what to do. I had to do something, so on the way back to my bedroom I grabbed a towel which I threw over the TV. It stayed that way for months before I dared watch it again. Even then, I was always nervous in case I saw the angry face once more.

Many other things happened to me at that house in Etwall as I was growing up, and later I worked as a tour guide at a famous haunted castle, so I got really used to experiencing unusual things.

I now live in my parents' house with my own family. My daughter has my old room, and she sometimes feels uncomfortable in there, but she will not talk about it. I try to remain open to her and reassure her that nothing is there that will hurt her.

A HORSE TRACE – CASTLETON

When I was at school I went on a trip to the YHA near Castleton. About a week before the trip my friend had given me a book about the most haunted places in Derbyshire and I was fascinated by it, so I took it with me on the trip.

There was a chapter in the book about the youth hostel, and it said that one of the former landowners had died and his wife had subsequently died of a broken heart. Ever since, according to the book, people have seen her riding a black horse across the hills.

The next morning we left the hostel to explore the nearby caverns, but before we set off something caught my attention from the corner of my eye. I turned my head and saw a shadow flash, lasting about five seconds. According to the book on the paranormal, that is a sure sign of ghostly activity. It looked as if the shadow was coming out of the trees and it was like the head of a horse, a black horse, with blood red eyes and a beautiful black mane.

Ever since then I have wanted to return to watch at dawn for the heartbroken wife on her black horse. Hopefully I can see it for real next time.

STANDING IN THE CORNER – MICKLEOVER

One dark and stormy night a friend and I were sitting in my living room in my home in Mickleover, playing computer games with all of the lights off. Because the storm was not easing off, my friend asked if he could stay over on the settee, and I agreed.

We finished playing and I went upstairs to get a sleeping bag for my friend, when suddenly I heard him scream. I raced downstairs to see what was the matter. I burst through the door to the lounge, and there, in the half-lit room, I saw something that frightened the life out of me.

On the other side of the room I saw what looked like a little boy. He was looking at my friend, and had caused him to scream. Then all of a sudden the boy just faded away.

There was no way that either of us were staying in that house, so I grabbed my sleeping bag, risked the storm and spent the night at my friend's house instead. I only returned once a priest had been in and blessed my home.

ALONE IN THE HOUSE – CHADDESDEN

A few years ago I was alone in my house in Chaddesden. Well, I suppose I was not completely alone as my dog was in the house to keep me company. I was watching TV, with my dog curled up next to me, when suddenly the lights flickered and went out, and so did the television.

Naturally I assumed a fuse had blown, so I grabbed a torch and went to the cellar, where the fuse box was. My dog followed at my heels, and as I swung the torch around, trying to locate the fuse box, I became aware that she was growling at a spot under the stairs. Curious, I took a look at where she was barking, and there in the darkness I saw a set of glowing red eyes.

I fled up the stairs, horrified, but before I could get through the door from the cellar it slammed shut in my face. I ran back downstairs, and then I tripped and fell. As I lay helpless on the floor, with my dog yapping beside me, I felt the thing under the stairs approach me. I was terrified and shut my eyes tight. Then, before I knew it, the lights came back on and the thing with red eyes was gone.

WINDOW MAN – DERBY

I was sitting on a sofa in my cousin's house one day and I felt a cold sweep of air go past me. I turned around really fast, thinking that my cousin was playing a prank, but no one was there.

Later that same evening, when all of my cousin's family were sitting down watching *Most Haunted*, we heard a clatter come from the empty kitchen. I got up to investigate and saw that the ice cream and fallen out of the freezer and skidded to the far side of the kitchen which I thought was a faulty door perhaps.

A couple of hours later I was still sitting on the sofa, huddled up on my own, when all of a sudden I thought I heard rustling in the kitchen. As I looked over, thinking it was probably only my cousin but also wanting to make sure that it was not the dodgy freezer playing up again, to my horror I saw the figure of a man reflected in the window. I ran into my cousin's room, where she was practising her guitar and I told her, as calmly as I could, to come and sit with me in the living room. Although a little puzzled, my cousin agreed. Then, as we left her bedroom, she looked down the hallway and saw the old man. I saw her check in front of me and so I peered past her to see what had caused her to become frozen to the spot. As I looked I felt a chill up my back, which developed into pure terror when the figure slowly disappeared in front of us.

After we had calmed down, we told each other not to be frightened and went to bed. I eventually got to sleep, but awoke suddenly when I heard something whisper 'get up' in my ear. I quickly opened my eyes and looked around my room to see if anyone was there, but I saw nothing. Then, before I really had chance to be scared, I saw the most beautiful sunrise ever pouring its light through the window.

My cousin and I decided to investigate the house's history to see if it could shed some light on our ghostly experiences. Eventually we tracked down the house's old owner, who said that her dad died in the room where I had stayed and apparently he used to love getting up early and watching the sunrise in the morning.

THE TWISTING OF THE DOORKNOB - DERBY

One night I was lying in my top bunk watching TV and started getting a bit tired, so I climbed down to turn off my set. However, before I got to the floor I heard my door handle turn. I thought it was my sister, so I decided to jump out on her and scare her. I jumped down off the bunk, opened the door as fast as I could and shouted boo, but no one was there. I leaned out of the room but again saw no one. I shouted to my sister, but I was sure that it was not her because I would have heard her run back into her room. I could hear everything through the wall; her TV, voice, footsteps, everything. Still confused, I went to speak to her about what had happened and she said she thought it was me trying to freak her out.

I went downstairs for a bit to watch TV and clear my mind and did not go back to bed until about 5am. I closed my door, got into my top bunk, and glanced over at the door, then as I did so I heard the noise of my doorknob again, but this time the door began to open. I sat up, petrified, and as the door slowly swung open I saw the scariest thing I had ever seen.

A figure stood in the doorway with no eyes and no feet. As it looked into my bedroom my heart was racing and I froze in terror. I closed my eyes, hoping it would go, and when I dared to open them again, it had gone.

MUSIC BOX - DERBY

I have a beautiful music box that was given to me by my mother when she cleared out her house one year. She told me that she bought it from an antique fair at Kedleston Hall.

When I opened the box later that day a beautiful song started to play. Then weirdly I felt someone hugging me and playing with my hair. However, I did not feel alarmed or scared. Sensing that it was standing behind me, I turned around and saw a little girl, about six years old, smiling. I should probably point out that I have always been able to see spirits and so I was not scared at all and instead simply tried talking to her.

I saw that she had long, white-blonde hair that went down to her waist and wore a white nightgown. She smiled and waved at me, and I did the same back. She told me her name was Mary Elizabeth and that the music box had belonged to her, and she was happy that it now belonged to me. I thanked her, and she smiled and disappeared.

I reflected for a moment and was happy that I met this girl as I had never had such a clear and pleasant encounter with a spirit before.

I later asked my sister to take a picture of me with the music box on her mobile phone, and to our amazement when we viewed the photo there was a little girl with long, blonde hair, hugging me and playing with my hair.

THE FACE AT THE WINDOW - ABBEY STREET, DERBY

One night when I was a child I was alone in my house in Abbey Street, Derby, as my parents had not yet come in from work. I was watching TV, when suddenly the lights and TV switched off. As I sat there in the dark, wondering what to do, I heard the sound of screaming, which filled the entire house.

I was petrified, to say the least, and I had no idea what to do. I just sat there in the chair for what seemed like hours, and when my parents finally came home they found me still shaking.

I finally snapped out of my state of shock and told them what had happened, and to try and calm me down they told me it must have been animals or something outside.

Later that night I heard something like the panting of an animal coming from outside my bedroom window, so I crept out of bed to check it out. I was shaking as I slowly pulled back my curtains, and there, inches away from the other side of the window, I saw a man in a hooded coat with glowing blue eyes. He did not have a nose or mouth, just a pair of horrible eyes.

I screamed so loudly that it woke my mum and dad, who came running into the room. However, when they looked out of the window there was nothing there. There may not have been anything there when they looked, but I know I did not imagine the whole thing.

THE CINEMA GHOST - GREEN LANE, DERBY

A few years ago my girlfriend's parents went on holiday and my girlfriend, her brother and I looked after the house for them. To thank us, when they got back they decided to pay for us to go to the cinema.

We searched through the listings and chose a classic film showing at the cinema on Green Lane in Derby and that evening we made our way to the cinema, bought our tickets and sat down in the auditorium. Once I was settled, I looked around and saw that the cinema was almost empty – maybe the film was not that much of a classic after all. The lights went dim and the movie began.

Then, out of the corner of my eye, I saw someone sitting in our row that I had not noticed previously. I turned to look and there, just a few feet away, I saw the figure was a girl whom I could clearly see straight through, and she was looking over the shoulder of a couple of girls in the aisle in front. The girl was definitely wearing a suit, which seemed a little out of place. I turned away to ask my girlfriend if she could see her, but when we both looked back the girl had disappeared.

FIRE FACE - ASHBOURNE

One cold January night I was sitting in front of the open fire in my parents' house in Ashbourne. It felt good to be at home doing nothing for a change as I was studying to become a chef and my life was really hectic.

I stretched myself out in front of the fire and enjoyed being alone as my brother was upstairs.

Then, to my surprise, a loud pop came from the fire and sparks flew from the fireplace. My brother, who had heard me yelp in alarm, ran out of his room to see if I was okay. I assured him I was and he went back into his room.

No sooner had my brother left the room, the fire gave out a loud roar and sparks poured out of the logs. The fire flickered a lot and I looked closely into it, mesmerised. As I gazed into the raging flames I saw something that still chills me to this day: the big face of a grotesque monster formed in the fire. I froze in fear, and the face growled and roared. It looked deformed and it had long horns. I found my voice and yelled out a scream, and it did the same. My brother ran out of his room and into the lounge again, just as the face seemed to leap forwards out of the fire.

'Say a prayer!' My brother shouted, and we both said the Lord's Prayer. Then, as we ended the prayer the face slowly faded away into the fire, and my brother and I just sat there, gasping.

CHAPTER 2

POLTERGEIST ACTIVITY

Many people get very frightened when they hear the word poltergeist as it conjures up images of terribly frightening events and sinister paranormal events. However, not all poltergeist activity would be at home on a Hollywood set, as it can be very subtle.

There are many explanations as to what a poltergeist is, but I personally believe that it is caused by self-induced psychokinesis, rather than it being a malevolent spirit.

The word 'poltergeist' is made up from two words, both of which are Germanic in origin. The first one – poltern – means 'to knock', and the second one – geist – means 'spirit'. Poltergeist is often translated as 'knocking ghost' or 'noisy ghost'. However, today the term is generally used to describe spontaneous psychokinesis, caused by psychological or emotional disturbances and mental changes in both adults and teenagers, and this tends to be the modern theory on poltergeist activity that is believed by paranormal researchers.

Research has suggested that teenagers cause most poltergeist activity, and in most cases the individual is not aware that they are the cause of these disturbances.

PAGES TURNING – SHARDLOW

My grandmother used to own an old house just outside Shardlow, which has since been knocked down and many people in my family had terrible experiences in that house.

One example involved my mother and her partner who were spending the night the house. As there was no TV my mother had taken a magazine to pass the time. She later fell asleep at around 11pm, but was woken up by the sound of something rustling. She became more and more frightened as she listened to the noise, and looked around to try and see what was causing it.

Her heart began to race as she saw that the pages of her magazine were turning rhythmically, as if someone was reading it. She woke up her partner but by the time he was awake enough to grasp what my mum was saying, the page turning had stopped.

A couple of years later my mother was talking to a cousin who had lived in the house and she found out that the pages of her cousin's school textbooks would turn by themselves, too. I can tell you that nobody in the family was upset when the house was knocked down!

AFTER THE BONE – DERBY

I encountered a poltergeist when I was only 12 years old. It all started after I found an old bone in my back yard. I found it fascinating and decided to keep it, and that was when things started to go wrong.

The following afternoon I walked home from Cavendish School, then went to my room, as I always did, where I saw my saxophone sitting on my bed, straight up. I was stunned; there was nothing holding it in that position. Then things got even stranger. I walked into a room to find a lamp upside-down on the table. At about midnight that night, I woke up and saw my fan had been turned on, so I got out of bed and crept over to switch it off, but when I got there I saw that the switch was already set to the 'off' position.

More things began to happen in the house soon after. My sister told me that one night she woke up to see her doll walking on her bed. That was the final straw for my parents and we ended up moving house. I left the bone in the backyard where I found it, and I have never been back to that house since.

THE RING – DERBY

In 1994 I was with a friend in my living room and a lamp suddenly started flickering next to her. A split second later we saw a pair of curtains that were lying on a table in front fly up into the air then drop back onto the table with a loud bang. Then an arc of white light swung up about 2ft away from us and disappeared through the ceiling, going right to left across our line of vision. We both just sat there in shocked silence.

It was the first time anything that dramatic and violent happened in that house, and to this day I have no idea what – or maybe even who – it was.

POKER TABLE PURSUIT

A little while ago my mum, two aunties and I went up to Scotland to visit my grandma. As it was a long drive from Derby we had decided to stay for a few nights.

The adults were playing poker in the living room one night while I was watching TV when all of a sudden the poker table started shaking and vibrating, and then it actually started moving towards me. I was so scared and backed away from it, and although I kept running it moved faster and continue following me. Everyone was screaming in the room.

I ran out of the living room as fast as I could and locked myself in my bedroom. It felt as if some kind of entity had followed me in there. My clothes started flying everywhere, my lamp switched on and off, and then it just stopped, as suddenly as it had all begun. There was silence. I opened the door, wanting to creep back to my mum, and saw the table was right outside the door. It jolted forwards and hit me. As I stood there, rubbing my knee and completely terrified, it seemed to go still again. Nothing happened after that, but I never went to grandma's after that.

NIGHTMARE ON ELM STREET - DERBY

In spring 1985 my fiancé Paul and I purchased a little terrace house on Elm Street, which was going to be our first home together when we married in July of that year. Paul decided to live in the house while I carried on living with my parents as I did not believe in living together before we were wed. We spent every penny and bit of spare time decorating and making the house into a home, and I could not wait to move in.

One day I had been shopping in Derby, buying things to furnish the house, and when I returned to my parents' house I wanted to tell Paul of all my purchases, so I decided to telephone him as I knew he was at our new home. I dialled the number and was surprised when an old woman answered the phone. I knew it could not be Paul's family as they lived quite far away, so I was very confused as to whom she was.

I asked to speak to Paul and she told me that she lived alone in the house. I apologised quickly and told her that I must have dialled the wrong number. She asked me what number I wanted and so I repeated the number back to her, and to my amazement she told me that I had dialled correctly.

I was starting to get panicky as the lady begged me to stay on the line. She was clearly lonely and I didn't want to offend her, but I wanted to speak to Paul. Unable to understand why I couldn't get through to him I decided to ask her where she lived, and I certainly wasn't prepared for her answer. She told me that her name was Maggie and she lived on Elm Street and proceeded to tell me the number. It was my house!

I slammed the receiver down and tried the number again, but this time Paul answered. I babbled some questions at him and he told me he was alone in the house and that he had been in all day.

I ran round to the house in a blind panic, totally confused. The house felt calming and surprisingly I did not feel any fear on entering it. I told Paul all about the old woman on the phone and he was as dumbfounded as I was.

Many years later I asked a neighbour who had lived in our house previously about the history of the property, and I was told that an old lady called Maggie who worked as a medium had lived there for many years. I do not know why she decided to contact me that day but I felt safe when I moved in to the house as though Maggie was keeping a watchful eye over us.

TEA FOR TWO – DERBY

In 1986 I worked as a shop assistant in C&A in Derby. I loved my job but in the run up to Christmas I was always rushed off my feet as customers tried to bag a bargain, and each day I would be willing the clock to home time.

One evening in November I returned home to find that the house was freezing cold, so I checked all the radiators, but to my surprise I found that they were working fine. I put the gas fire on in the lounge but it made little difference to the temperature.

I wandered into the kitchen and decided to make myself a cup of tea, as I did each night when I returned home from work. I took a mug off the mug tree and placed a tea bag inside then went back into the lounge to see if it had warmed up while I waited for the kettle to boil. On returning to the kitchen, I found that there were now two mugs with teabags in sitting on the work surface. Convinced that I must have taken two mugs down by mistake, I returned one to the mug tree and placed the tea bag back inside the caddy before fetching the milk from the fridge. I only turned my back for a few seconds, but when I turned round there were two mugs on the work surface again. Again I placed the tea bag and mug back in their rightful places, turned away to place the milk back inside the fridge, and when I turned around to get my drink, there was another one, complete with hot water and a tea bag in!

I lived on my own, so I knew nobody was playing jokes on me, but I could not for the life of me understand how it got there. I began to go over the possibilities in my head. If it had simply fallen off the mug tree I would have heard it fall, and the possibility of it falling upright was zero. Also, the tea bags were kept in a caddy with a tight screw lid, and I would have certainly heard water being poured from a kettle! Just as I was considering the puzzling events I saw a white mist appear in front of me in the kitchen.

Fear caused me to shout out, 'OK, if you want a cup of tea, you can have one!' I ran back into the lounge feeling scared and confused, but no sooner had I shouted the words, I felt the temperature in my home start to rise until it was breathlessly hot, and so I quickly turned off the fire and central heating. That done, I cautiously made my way back to the kitchen.

To be honest, I was rather disappointed to find that the additional cup of tea in the kitchen had not been drunk when I re-entered. But to this day I am convinced that I encountered a ghost.

A NIGHT TO REMEMBER - KEDLESTON ROAD, DERBY

It was raining heavily outside and I decided to stay in my flat on Kedleston Road and watch a scary film. I have always loved horror movies and that night I decided to watch *The Exorcist*. The film finished at about midnight and afterwards I turned off my lights and went to bed. I was just settling down when, suddenly, my bed started to shake. At first I just thought it was dream brought on by watching the film.

However, my bed started to shake even more wildly, and I knew that it was no nightmare. I wanted to turn on the lights to see if I could figure out what was happening but for some reason I could not move one inch of my body. I tried to kick my legs and move my arms, but it felt as if something was holding me down.

I tried to scream, but then it felt as if someone was choking me. I was petrified, screaming inside my head with my pulse humping in my ears. I completely gave up resisting and opened my eyes but nothing was there.

I turned on my lights and heard a strange, howling scream. It scared me to death once again, so I turned off the lights, dived under the duvet and lay there until morning. I have never watched that movie again.

TERRIFYING TOYS – CODNOR

I loved it when my grandson came to stay with my husband and I in Codnor, and I always made sure that we had lots of fun things planned so that he enjoyed his visits.

One weekend my son and daughter-in-law dropped off Simon, my grandson, along with his mountain of carrier bags containing a range of toys to keep him occupied. They were thankful for a weekend alone as Simon was not the quietest of children and had the energy of a whirlwind.

After an afternoon of playing it was time to put Simon to bed. He slept in my son's old room, and I carried all his toys into the room.

For the rest of the evening I could not shake a strange feeling of dread that something unpleasant was going to happen. I decided to read for a bit as my husband was snoring loudly besides me, but just as I was getting into my book I heard a door bang and then footsteps coming up the stairs. Almost frozen with fear thinking we had an intruder I woke up my husband and whispered to him what I had just heard.

My husband jumped out of bed and told me to stay put, but after nearly 40 years of marriage I was not about to start doing as I was told, so I followed him and grabbed a candlestick which stood on my dressing table as I passed.

We crept downstairs together and searched the whole house, but we couldn't find anything out of place so we returned to bed. As soon as we got into bed we heard a door slam again and the room had a sudden icy chill running through it. I started to get very frightened but decided that Simon's safety was the most important thing, so I jumped out of bed and decided to check on him.

On entering Simon's room my husband and I both felt the most incredible gust of cold air, and there, standing upright in the middle of the room, were his Action Men, and their arms and legs were moving. Neither my husband nor I could ever be described as believers in the paranormal and would have scorned this very story if we had not seen it with our own eyes.

We stood there, fixed to the spot, and as I glanced at Simon I could see he had also witnessed this strange event. He was sitting up in bed, staring wide-eyed at his toys. I ran across the room and held him.

'Grandma, they are moving on their own, I have been watching them for ages but I was too scared to scream.' Simon cried as he clung on to me for dear life.

My husband, although not a religious man, suddenly shouted the Lord's Prayer out loud, and as he did so the toys stood still. He then picked them up and threw them out of the window into the garden. As soon as he had done this the temperature in the room returned to normal.

I am not sure what happened that night, and to be honest I don't think I really want to know, but all I can say is that I know what I saw and as a result my grandson no longer plays with Action Men or stays over at our house.

MOVING WITH THE TIMES – CHADDESDEN

I fell in love with my house in Chaddesden as soon as I saw it and could not wait to move in on 15 December 1997. It was my first home since I got divorced and marked my new independence. I loved living there and soon made a lot of friends in the area, and for the first time in many years I believed that my life was finally back on track.

After a short while I decided to have some work done at the house and started with the removal of a very dated gas fire in the lounge. The plumber removed it and discovered that I had a lovely big open chimney behind it, and he advised me that it would look lovely with a simple log basket in it.

Within a few weeks my new open fire was ready to use and all that was left for me to do was redecorate the room, so I decided to take a week off work to get it done. The first thing that I did was move the sofa into the middle of the room, which was not an easy task as the thing was so heavy, then I went into the hall to fetch some dust sheets. But when I returned to the living room I found, to my utter amazement, that the sofa was back in its original place. Thinking that I must have imagined I had moved it, I pushed the sofa into the middle of the room and immediately covered it with the sheets.

A few hours later, after stripping off the old wallpaper, I was ready to do some gloss painting, so I put the white gloss and paintbrush on the mantel, but before starting I went into the kitchen to make myself a cup of tea. On my return I could not find the tin of gloss paint anywhere. I knew for certain that I had put it on the mantel so that I wouldn't knock it over, and although I searched high and low for it I could not find it anywhere. I had no alternative but to go and buy some more from B&Q.

After my unplanned shopping trip, I arrived home opened the tin of paint, moaning to myself that I was way behind schedule and saw the original tin of paint was back on the mantel, exactly where I had left it. I really couldn't believe my eyes.

There were many other incidents that occurred when I decorated the room; from wallpaper mysteriously hanging itself on opposite sides of the room, to the wallpaper paste going missing just after I had mixed it up.

I don't know what or who was trying to prevent me from finishing the decorating, but what I do know is that I had no experiences before I removed the old fire, so I wonder if I upset the spirit of someone who had chosen the fire by having it removed.

CHAPTER 3

STRANGE BUT TRUE!

This is a fascinating chapter in which you will find a collection of strange stories covering everything from time-warps to UFOs.

THE PHOTOGRAPH – DERBY

My family and I moved into a lovely new house built on the land that had belonged to Aston Hospital. The house had a lovely feel about it and we were glad that after years of renting we had somewhere we could call our own.

Just as we were getting settled my husband was made redundant, and then two weeks later I found out I was expecting another baby. We were worried sick trying to work out how we were going to cope financially. Days out were a thing of the past already and we had to watch every penny.

One day soon afterwards I saw a sign for a local car boot sale, and my husband and I decided that it would be good to take the kids there to have a browse around. It was also a cheap day out and a distraction from our financial worries.

On the day of the sale we got up early, wrapped ourselves up as the weather that day was not particularly kind, and walked the short distance to the sale. There was a good turn out on that Sunday and we went from car to car in the hope that we would find a bargain or a hidden treasure among the usual old baby things and unwanted records.

We were nearing the end when an old photograph in a gilt frame of an elderly couple caught my eye. It was not a particularly pretty picture and the couple were not smiling in it, but nevertheless I felt really drawn to it. Unfortunately, my husband and children did not share my enthusiasm, yet for some reason I knew I just had to have it and take it home.

I placed the photograph on my Welsh dresser, and I even jokingly named the couple Wilf and Betty. Every morning from then on when I walked past the dresser I would say good morning to them.

One morning, after my usual greeting to them, I grabbed the mountain of bills that I had piled up on top of the Welsh dresser.

'Oh Betty, what are we going to do with all these?' I heard myself saying to the battered old photograph. Just then I felt the strangest sensation, which I can only describe as a warm cuddle. I was bathed in its warmth, and suddenly the newspaper fell off the table and lay open on the job page. I bent down to pick it up and I heard a loud voice in my head shout 'look 48'. Somehow I knew that the voice was instructing me to turn to page 48, so I quickly did and as I found the page a job advert seemed to jump out. I sat down and read it, and realised it was ideal for my husband. I showed it to him, and he applied for the job straight away – and got it!

After that we started to make real progress with our finances, and we were just getting back on our feet when the car broke down and we needed £200 to get it fixed. We simply did not have the spare cash and our baby was due any day, so it could not have come at a worse time. Again I found myself cursing our misfortune as I was dusting the photograph. Then, as loud as before, I heard the words 'scratch card' in my head. The words played over in my mind and I decided to walk to the local paper shop to purchase one.

Heavily pregnant and breathless, I felt a bit silly but I felt compelled to listen to the voice.

As I started to scratch off the silver panel I felt the strange warm cuddle feeling again and somehow I knew things would be alright. I looked at the scratch card and discovered that I had won £200!

Over the next few years, whenever I needed a little bit of help I would go and ask the photograph and they always seemed to deliver and I was always mindful to thank them.

As our children started to grow, we decided to move house. I packed our things away ready for the move, and on the day that we were due to leave I wrapped the photograph in bubble wrap and made sure that I marked the box carefully. When we got to the new house and unpacked the boxes, however, I could not find the photograph anywhere. The whole family searched for hours to find it, but it had simply vanished. From that day, I have never heard the voice in my head or had the luck that we had before.

CLOSE ENCOUNTERS - BOSTOCKS LANE

My wife worked at Risley Park Nursing Home and always worked afternoons. I left with my son at nine o'clock to pick her up each day as she finished at half past. We lived in Kirk Hallam, Ilkeston, and so we travelled through the old Stanton Ironworks along the country lanes, which brought us out at Bostocks Lane.

One night, on 14 October 1995 to be exact, the area felt really odd as we were travelling along the country lanes. I could feel the hairs standing up on the back of my neck and I knew that something wasn't right. I just could not place what. Then, all of a sudden, a blue electric current flooded across one of the farmers' fields between Stanton Ironworks and Bostocks Lane. There was no thunder in the sky that night; it was just an ordinary cold British night. I had never seen anything like it before, it was like something out of a Hollywood movie, and my son and I were speechless for about five minutes.

When we got to the nursing home to pick up my wife, I explained what I'd just seen and she looked as shocked as we felt. After all, why would a father and son make anything like this up?

I felt privileged to have witnessed this strange event, believing that I would never see anything like that ever again. How wrong I was.

A few weeks later we left the house as usual to fetch my wife. We were travelling past the old entrance to Stanton Ironworks, towards the bend in the road just before the Stanhope Arms pub, when all of a sudden my son and I saw something that will stay with us for the rest of our lives. There, in the sky above us, was a huge triangular shape, which was covered in red lights and just hovered in the sky and revolved as it gracefully flew past.

I slammed the brakes on at this point and found myself staring open mouthed at what had to be a flying saucer. It was not a light in the distant sky as it was at most 500ft above the car, and both my son and I could see it perfectly clearly. I was excited and full of adrenalin, but at the same time I was petrified because I knew the stories about alien abductions.

I told my wife about our sighting but she did not believe me this time – in fact nobody ever has. A few weeks later a television programme called *Schofield's Quest*, which was presented by Philip Schofield, mentioned that there had been sightings in the Derbyshire area at the same time that we had witnessed our sighting so I am totally convinced it was real.

PHANTOM VOICES – DERBY

One early autumn day last year, I was arriving home from work and the sun was just above the horizon. It was a warm evening, and several of the neighbours were working on their lawns or washing their cars.

As I was waiting for the garage door to open, my mobile phone rang. It was my husband calling to let me know he was running late leaving work but was on his way. After parking the car in our garage, still talking on the phone with my husband, I entered the house through a door which connects the garage to our hall. Our house is a split-level, with steps leading to the living area and then more stairs up to the bedrooms. As always (I have seen too many scary movies), I turned on the lights in the hall before I entered.

Suddenly, I heard the oddest sounds coming from the upstairs bedroom area: a male voice, a female voice and a baby's cry. I was afraid because I knew no one was in the house. The hairs on the back of my neck stood up and my heart pounded.

I was still on the phone to my husband, so I told him to be quiet as I tried to explain what was happening, but he thought I was joking or hearing things. I stood still and strained to hear, then I heard a sound coming from the basement like a TV was on. I turned the corner to the top of the cellar stairs, and from the top step I could see that the TV down there was off. I was shaking as I was certain that I had heard noises coming from the set. I could not stand being inside any more, so I walked out and sat down on a bench in the front garden, still on the phone to my husband.

He kept saying I was crazy, but I know what I heard.

WOMAN IN THE CASTLE - DERBY

Twenty-two years ago my husband left me for another woman. I was so broken hearted that I had gone off food and had lost a lot of weight and with three small children it was an enormous struggle.

One night I dreamt that I was being led through a lush, green field. The person guiding me was invisible, but I could hear them speaking. I knew they were walking alongside me, but I couldn't see them. The person in my dream led me to a castle, and we walked up stone steps until we reached the top floor. I was faced with a huge oak door, and my guide made it open.

In the room I saw a woman with clear blue eyes and she looked to be around 30. She had blonde hair piled on her head, as was the style at the beginning of the previous century. Her crimson-coloured dress was also from the Victorian era. She was wearing a ring with an enormous ruby.

She waved me to her, so I walked over, and she looked me in the eye and said, 'I am your mother's sister. I am always here and will always be with you.' Then at that moment I woke up. With tears in my eyes I rang my mother and told her about the dream.

She came over to my house immediately and asked if the woman resembled any of her sisters, as she had four. I said 'Yes, the eldest,' and proceeded to describe her. My mother smiled. She said that I had described her sister to the last detail. My mother was glad she was looking after me in that time of trouble and from that day on my life changed for the better.

THREE ODDITIES IN ONE NIGHT – DERBYSHIRE DALES

My friends and I once went camping in the Derbyshire Dales. We are seasoned travellers, but even so on arriving at our destination the wind and rain were so heavy that we decided to find a hotel for the night rather than brave a tent.

It was a very old hotel, but recent renovations made it look new. It was rather intimidating when we first arrived as not many people were staying there and it seemed to have an eerie feeling about it. As the weather worsened we decided to stay there for our entire holiday; a creepy hotel was surely better than a soaking tent.

On the second night of our stay we were in the lobby and were enjoying telling each other stories, when suddenly, out of the blue, what looked like an orb flew past us. We thought it was just our eyes playing a trick on us and it was soon forgotten. A little while later my friend suggested that we go and take a walk in the woods, so we left the hotel and made our way to some local woodland. As we approached the tree line one of my friends and I saw something unbelievable – the shadow of a woman came out of the trees towards us. We were so scared by the sight that we decided to rush straight back to our hotel and the others soon followed once they saw how shaken we were.

In my room that night we had another fright when one of my friends wanted to go to the toilet. The door seemed to be locked from the inside and we could see that the light was on through a chink in the door. I tried to turn the knob, and suddenly it clicked open by itself. However, no one was inside.

We decided that was enough and we left the very next day!

WREATH OF FEATHERS - SINFIN

After World War Two my parents came to England from Poland and settled in Derby. My dad was a proud man and considered himself fortunate to have been able to set up home in the city with my mother, and so they worked hard all their lives. Just living in Derby made him feel like a king compared to the lifestyle his own parents had had in Poland.

My mother was a cleaner and had three jobs to fit in around my school hours, while my father was a bus driver and worked shifts, so it was very rare that the two of them were home at the same time except on a Sunday.

I can remember coming home from my primary school in Sinfin one day to find my father at home and my mother at work, and I can remember how excited I was to spend some quality time with him. He poured me some warm milk and sat me on his knee, ready to tell me some stories from his homeland. I had never been to Poland, yet I am very proud that I am Polish even if I do not speak a word of the native tongue.

My father started to tell me a story about his mother, who had passed away many years before I was born. Yet from his rich descriptions it felt as though I had known her.

He started to tell me about when she died, and that just before she had taken her last breath she had told my grandfather that the angels had come to take her home. She died minutes later, and when the doctor came to examine her she was clutching a tiny, perfectly formed wreath of white feathers, which everyone was certain had not been there before. My father explained to me that if you have been good in life when you die the angels place a wreath of feathers in your hand to help you on your journey to heaven. It gave me a warm feeling inside knowing that my gran must have been such a good woman that the angels were with her, and I wished that I would see such a wreath of feathers.

Although my father told me many stories throughout my childhood, the one about the wreath of feathers stuck with me, and I would say that it was the root of my fascination with angels, although I had never been lucky enough to see one.

Throughout my life I have called on the angels to help me and I often find single white feathers, which I believe to be signs that the angels are with me. However, although I worked in a nursing home and have held the hands of many dying people I had never seen a wreath of feathers.

Later my mother became seriously ill and by September 2000 she was dying from cancer, and my father and I kept our promise and cared for her at home, with the help of the Macmillan nurses. One overcast Monday, Sue, the nurse, told me that she felt it would not be long before my mother passed away as she had taken a turn for the worse over the weekend. She advised me to bathe my mother and then sit with her and hold her hands. My father and I sat down next to my mother as her favourite song played on the stereo. She looked beautiful that morning, with her hair freshly done, and I sensed that she was happy. All of a sudden the room filled with brilliant sunshine, just like on a summer's day. It illuminated the whole room and there seemed to be a tingle in the air and that very second my mother took her last breath.

My father, Sue and I cried, yet at the same time I felt relieved that she was no longer suffering, which gave me some comfort. I bent forward and kissed her on the forehead, and as I did so I noticed something in her hands. I opened her fingers to take a closer look and to my astonishment found a small, perfect wreath of white feathers. It was made of 11 snow-white feathers, each one intertwined with the next. I asked my father and Sue if they had placed it there and they said not, and by the looks on their faces I knew they were telling the truth. As much as I wanted to keep the wreath of feathers, I decided that it should be buried with my mother as it was a gift from the angels to her. I just hope that when I pass away, I get the special gift too.

MY SON HEARD – ELVASTON CASTLE

About nine years ago, when my eldest child was three, my husband and I used to take him for long rides in the car, and one of our favourite places to go was Elvaston Castle. It is a beautiful place full of green trees and well-manicured grounds.

One warm summer's day we arrived at the castle and I realised that I had never visited the church in the grounds, so we decided to visit it. I was disappointed to find that the church doors were locked but decided to have a look around the graveyard instead as I have a morbid fascination with very old graves.

My son was in his pushchair and my husband was pushing him as the ground was very uneven. We stopped on a piece of grass which did not seem to have any tombstones on and was very overgrown and my son started getting agitated. I asked him what was wrong and he said

'Mummy, I don't like it here anymore. I can hear the babies in the ground crying!'

My husband and I just looked at each other, stunned. I know children are supposed to be sensitive to the supernatural, but my son also has Asperger's disorder, which is a form of autism. One of the effects of the condition is that the sufferer cannot lie. They have no concept of it because they cannot deal in the abstract. We left the graveyard as fast as we could, scared by what our son had said.

My son is 12 now, and, believe it or not, he still to this day insists that he heard those poor babies crying.

THE TOOTH - DERBY

My story begins with the creation of a fledgling ghost-hunting society, started by myself and two others from Derby University about eight years ago.

We used to drive to locations that we had heard stories about and walk around them in the hope of witnessing something paranormal. Most of the time we just ended up scaring ourselves, but on one occasion we encountered something more than we had bargained for.

One night we were walking up Burton Road, exploring a mansion where a man had hung himself. Local school kids had been going to the abandoned house for many years, drinking beer on the porch and generally freaking themselves out. All sorts of stories abounded of strange noises, cold spots and ghostly apparitions, and so we were determined to discover its secrets.

I always researched an area we were about to explore at the local library, so we would have an idea of what to expect and I would take along any hard evidence such as newspaper articles to show my friends.

While I was carrying out my research I discovered that the old house had a dark side to it. Rumours circulated of satanic rituals and other dark work being carried put there, and needless to say the rumours frightened me before we even got there.

As we walked towards the house Amy, a member of our group, became frightened too. As we continued onwards the clouds blocked out the moonlight and the night became extremely dark.

We approached a boarded-up house on the corner, which was in a serious state of disrepair but still standing. Graffiti was sprayed all over the boards covering the windows, and we knew the house had to be unoccupied.

We walked forward, and as we passed under the fence we saw an etching of a pentagram. The path ended at a little gate which was the entrance to the rear of the mansion, or so we thought. We hopped over the gate and set out down another long path that led into an overgrown garden. At this point my two friends became so afraid that they turned back but I felt strangely compelled to continue. The overgrown trees and bushes were like a tunnel and became so overgrown that I ended up having to crawl to get by, until it got so narrow I couldn't continue. I considered turning back, when suddenly the path opened up into a small clearing, but it was still very dark.

I looked around with my flashlight, not really knowing what I expected to see, when out of the corner of my eye I noticed something very strange. I swung the torch around and pointed it just in front of my feet. The ground had strange marks burned into it like long slashing lines.

In the centre of the clearing was a small pile of rocks. I went over to look closer, and on top of the rocks was an animal's canine tooth. It was about three to four inches long, including the root, and very white.

As I picked it up, I heard my friend frantically shouting at me over and over, which made me feel very scared and I began to hurry back.

Fear overtook me and in my panicked state I did not pay too much attention to what I was doing as I crashed back out of the garden. I finally emerged to find my friends waiting nervously outside the gate. I could tell that something had definitely spooked them while I had been gone.

As I approached I asked them what had happened, but none of them answered me. They gestured for me to get into the car and we sped away. Finally, once we were completely off the road, I got them to tell me what had happened.

After they walked out of the garden, leaving me to continue, they had explored around the entrance, where they saw a figure floating in and out of an upstairs window. They were all visibly shaken as they told me what they had witnessed.

Once I got home I went up to my room and got ready for bed. I was worn out by the evening's excitement. I took everything out of my pockets, and as I absent-mindedly flicked though the contents of my pocket I noticed the strange tooth that I had discovered earlier. In my panic I had pocketed it. I decided to keep it and set it on top of my stereo, and then I turned my stereo on and got in the shower.

I was not in there long before the music suddenly cut out. I finished my shower, thinking a power surge must have reset it. When I got out, however, I could smell smoke and hurried back into my room. To my horror I saw that the stereo was smoking! The display on the front was going crazy and smoke was pouring from the top, right underneath the tooth. I hurried over, unplugged the stereo and everything stopped. Shaken, I took the tooth outside and tossed it away. I eventually went to sleep feeling unnerved, but not until after I had prayed harder than I ever had before. Needless to say that was our last ghost hunt!

THE FLYING DOVE - BORROWASH

One day, a few summers ago, my brother Ryan and I went to the cemetery in Borrowash to visit my great-grandma Margaret, who was buried there in the year 2000. We usually go there once in a while to look at her beautiful grave, as we both miss her very much.

For some reason this day turned out to be very special. After my brother and I had visited her grave, we turned around to leave and a dove flew right in front of our faces. It scared us half to death, but we both felt that our great-grandma had something to do with it, and that comforted our nerves. I had never seen a pure white dove before, and to us it was a message of love and warmth so we know she is still with us.

TRIPPING THE NIGHT FANTASTIC - CHADDESDEN

One night I was walking into the bar at the pub in Chaddesden, when suddenly I felt a strange draft. I looked around to see if the windows or doors were open, but they were not. The cold air sent a shiver down my back and all the hairs on the back of my neck stood on end.

I carried on walking and got my drinks, and as I was walking back with them something hit me in the arm and sent a drink flying. At the same time I heard my name being spoken with a foreign accent. I span around, wanting to see who had bumped me, but no one was near me. I was completely puzzled. A kind lady cleaned up the spilt drink and got me another one.

I walked over to where my friends were sitting and sat down on a stool, but no sooner had I bent over the damn thing was pulled away from me and I ended up on the floor. Now, normally my friends and I would have found this type of prank hilarious, but my friends were nowhere near the stool on this occasion and so there was no possible explanation for how it had moved.

There were no more incidents after that – until I got up to leave the pub. I was just going out of the door when someone shouted in the strange accent again, 'I will get you, Rubi.'

To this day I don't know what had it in for me that night, but I am glad to report that they have not got me yet!

Forget-me-not – Derby

On 24 October 2008 I was at my mate's house in Derby for her birthday party and sleepover. We had a great night drinking in Derby then we went on to a club before returning to her parents' house. It was about 3am when we turned the lights out, but as we did not feel like sleeping we sat up chatting, then all of a sudden we saw what looked like an old woman in white walking towards us. We could just make her out in the dark and we all froze.

I blinked, trying to tell myself it was just my imagination, but she was still there when I opened my eyes. She said that she was going to leave us something, and then she disappeared. My friend scrambled out of bed and put the lights on, but we could not see any trace of the old woman.

The next morning none of us could stop talking about what we had seen the night before, until one of my friends screamed. There in the middle of the floor was a tiny bunch of artificial forget-me-nots, tied together with string. The strange thing was that we had searched the floor the night before and it certainly hadn't been there then.

The future is orange – Ockbrook

During the 1980s I was living with my parents at our home in Ockbrook. One night, I was lying in my bed fast asleep until I was woken by a bright light which flooded my bedroom from outside the window. It was so bright that it illuminated everything in my room, so I got up out of my bed to have a look out of the window. I opened the curtain, and there in front of me I saw a bright orange, glowing light ball hovering in the sky above. It seemed to be rotating and there was no sound coming from it. Convinced that I was looking at a UFO, I panicked and ran back into bed.

The next day I went to the barbers and picked up a local paper to read as I waited for my turn. Right across the paper I saw the headline that a UFO had been seen in Derbyshire and military aircraft had been called in to investigate. Thankfully, many people saw the UFO that night so I knew that I had not been dreaming.

HAVE YOU EVER BEEN FOLLOWED? - KILBURN

I have lived in several places in Derbyshire, and it seems that no matter where I move there is always some sort of ghost or entity in my home. I truly believe that this ghost or entity follows me, as I certainly don't believe that every home I move into is haunted!

When I lived in Matlock I was physically touched, occasionally pushed lightly and once I was shoved, and each time there was no one in the house but me.

I later left Matlock and moved to Whatstandwell, and after approximately three months in my new home I again began to experience the sensation of being touched. I would also often find that my microwave door, dishwasher and fridge had been opened when I was out of the kitchen.

Then, when I moved to my next house in Crich, knick-knacks would often be knocked onto the floor in the morning when I woke. I even began to feel a hand around my ankle or wrist when I was on the verge of falling asleep.

I got married a few years later and my new husband began to feel the same things, as well as the feeling of fingers brushing across his face or someone touching the top of his head. When we moved to Belper we experienced much of the same, except that we began to hear sounds like a heavy box falling to the floor or what sounded like window glass being smashed. Yet, strangely, each time we investigated there was nothing out of place.

We then moved to Kilburn, and the same paranormal activities happen here, too, except now we notice dark shadows out of the corner of our eyes, which never happened before. At first we dismissed it, but we soon found that our two cats would look up and stare at the same spot as if they too could see something moving.

Once I picked my cat up for comfort and began walking towards the doorway of the bedroom. I was going to go into the living room but as I approached the door my cat suddenly ran across my back and under my bed.

More recently, my husband saw someone pass the doorway as he was watching TV in the spare room. He called out, assuming it was me, but when I didn't answer he came to look for me and found me watching a film in our bedroom. When I asked what he wanted, he told me he had seen me pass the doorway, and when I told him I hadn't moved we both felt a chill.

My mother and husband both think I attract the supernatural. Whether this is true or not, I have no idea, but as the years move on the level of activity seems to increase. It is bizarre and inexplicable!

A RUDE AWAKENING - DERBY

One night, at around 2am, I awoke to the sound of my bedroom door being violently slammed shut. At first I thought it was the wind, but then it opened all the way and slammed shut again all by itself. I froze and the same thing happened about 10 times. I was terrified!

My brother ran in as he had heard all the banging and was coming to give me an earful, but he stopped in his tracks when he noticed that I was still in my bed, then he started to get scared too.

Ten minutes later my other two brothers came into my room and we were shaking as we explained what had happened.

The next night my eldest brother stayed in my room, while I was in my other brothers' room. At 2am, just like the previous night, it happened again. For the next three days the door continued to open and slam shut all by itself.

Finally my eldest brother had had enough and searched online for ways to get rid of ghosts, and we decided to try several of the methods. Thankfully, one of them must have worked because we never had any problems again.

TAKE IT AS A WARNING

I have lived in Derbyshire all my life and in the 1980s I worked on an oil rig in the North Sea, working several weeks on and several weeks off. Life on the oil rig was like living in a very closely knit community as there was nowhere to go once you had been dropped on the rig to do your shifts.

We often felt like we were not alone, but some of the lads say they saw an apparition. The strange thing was that whenever the apparition appeared there was always an accident, which involved someone being injured or killed, and we began to see the apparition's appearance as a warning.

One day we were working on the rig when the apparition appeared before us. Stunned, we all wondered what was about to happen, and we did not have to wait long before a well exploded, but thankfully nobody was hurt. We were very relieved, as you can imagine, and we hoped that the curse of the apparition was now broken.

The very next day, however, one of the workmen went to repair the rig and was cutting some electrical wiring, and as he did this a spark came off his cutting tool and set alight a drum which was near him, causing a massive explosion that killed him outright.

BEAM ME UP SCOTTY! – DENBY

One day in January 2008 I was out walking my dog through Denby village. As I passed the old graveyard next to Denby Free School, all of a sudden I saw what I can only describe as a bright white light coming from one of the graves. It was the brightest light I have ever seen, and I although I was scared I felt compelled to find out what was causing the light, so I went through the gate and along the path to where it was shining.

Even though the sun was out, the grave itself was in shadow, and as I looked around to where the sun was shining through the trees I could see that it was more of a golden light, whereas the column of light coming from the grave was a definite white. It also had a more solid appearance and was coming straight up from the ground.

Out of curiosity I crept closer to the light, and my dog became agitated and started snarling. Normally I would have run away, but on this occasion fascination got the better of me and I reached out and try and touch the beam of light. As I put my hand out, slightly trembling with anticipation, the beam sort of moved away from my hand, then a bright red orb flew out of the beam and hovered in front of me. At this, my dog started to bark loudly and I felt it was time to go home, but as I turned to go I noticed, to my amazement, that the red orb was following me.

I kept turning around at regular intervals and saw that the red orb had followed me from the graveyard, all the way to Denby cricket ground, until it disappeared into thin air.

I have seen many strange things in my life, and even many orbs, but I have never seen a white beam of light coming from a grave or a red orb before, and unfortunately although I will it to show itself to me when I pass the graveyard I have never seen it since.

CAT NAPPING – SINFIN

About five years ago my great-grandmother's cat died from old age. She told me and my mother that the night after her cat had died, she felt her jump onto her bed and walk up to her head like she had always done. She knew her cat was saying goodbye. Me and my mum put this down to her age as she was 98 at the time, and I forgot all about it until my own cat died. My mum had got her two years before I was born and she lived to the age of 20, so I grew up with her and she slept on or in my bed every night.

A couple of nights after she died I was in bed reading under a low light when I felt a slight bounce at the foot of the bed. I looked up, and right before my eyes I watched paw prints appear all the way up my bed, along the side of my body. I was so scared when they got close to my head that I slipped myself out of bed and ran as fast as I could to my mum's room. However, she did not believe me and refused to go and look, but when I went back to my room the indentations were still visible.

Although I was scared at the time, I also felt strangely comforted after this happened, and I sometimes still wonder if my cat's ghostly presence is walking the streets every evening in Sinfin as she did when she was alive.

MORNING CONVERSATION – DERBY

My mother is a very no-nonsense person. Anything that cannot be backed up with a logical explanation, she disregards as nonsense. Black is black to her, and you make your own luck in life. She is well educated, having gained both a Masters degree and PhD, and that is why it is so hard not to believe her.

There was always something weird about my mother's first husband, the man she was married to before she met my father. Everybody described him as though he was not quite of this world. He was Scandinavian by birth and his parents were missionaries sent to another country. He had grown up in some small minimalist village, completely isolated from modern civilisation. Needless to say, he had an unusual upbringing. He was an artist and a truly unique soul. His name was Allen, and he saw the beauty in small things that you and I would probably overlook.

One day my mother went to her cousin's house for dinner with Allen. They had just arrived when a group of people were leaving the house, and one of them was a close friend of her cousin's husband, a man named Tony. They were introduced, and as Tony was walking away, my mother commented, 'Well, he seemed nice.' Allen immediately replied, 'Well, then, he can be your next husband.'

One morning soon afterwards my mother woke up early to find that Allen was already awake. He was sitting in the easy chair next to her bed, and they began to talk about the upcoming day. Something caught my mother's eye, and she looked to her side to see what it was, and Allen was asleep next to her. She looked back but to her surprise there was nobody in the chair. On a few other occasions, my mother apparently woke up in the middle of the night to find Allen floating an inch or two above the bed.

Not long after the dinner party at my mother's cousin's house, Allen died. A few years later my mother was at a wedding, where she happened to meet Tony again. Tony is my mother's second husband just as Allen had suggested. They settled in Derby, where I was born, and have been happily married for many years.

MALICIOUS SPIRIT – DUFFIELD

In April 2003 I was home alone for the weekend in my parents' house in Duffield. My parents were on holiday and my siblings were sleeping over at their friends' houses.

With a computer at hand I browsed some spiritual sites on the internet to satisfy my curiosity for the subject and to pass the time. I read about the ways of communicating and summoning spirits, and the danger of bad spirits and haunting. I was open minded, and I wanted to explore the concept a little further.

I discovered a site that explained a way to summon spirits via spells and reagents. Intrigued, I went down to a stall in the old Market Hall and bought a few purple candlesticks and some red ink to create some atmosphere.

On the Saturday night I drew some other weird symbols I had looked up. It said that they would have the same effect as a Ouija board and create a channel between the spirit world and ours. I placed the candles in three corners of the pattern of symbols and lit them.

I was, of course, hesitant for a moment. I recited a spell and once I finished, my gut hurt and the warmth of the room was siphoned away. The candles went out and then suddenly relit. Strange scratching sounds travelled along the walls, and I could sense a malicious presence. I got up to dash out of the room, when suddenly something grabbed my ankle and threw me face first to the floor.

I turned onto my back to look above me, which was a mistake, because I saw that the evil being was floating above me. In a sharp, long moment of pain, it felt like the thing was dripping acid onto my chest.

My clothing was not damaged but was drenched in blood – my blood. I felt my chest and it was covered in bleeding wounds.

I eventually managed to get up, and with a mad adrenalin rush I ran to the living room and grabbed the Bible. I recited John 3:16 over and over again, until the dark spirit was driven from me. I got courage from this and dared to enter the room that contained what I was convinced was a demon.

I recited John 3:16 again while I stepped closer to the triangle of candles. As I closed in, the candles burned like great torches and the flames filled the room with heat. I heard a scream unlike anything I have ever heard before, and as I stood over the triangle I yelled, 'By the name of God, Jesus and the Holy Spirit, I command you back to hell!'

I put the Bible into the triangle and forcibly held the pages open at John 3:16 as the demon tried to close it. Something like a shockwave crashed from underneath the Bible and knocked the candles over, ripping the pictures off the walls.

The air went fresh again and I blacked out, and when I woke up half an hour later my face was resting on the open pages of the Bible. The symbols I had drawn were all damaged beyond recognition, and the candles were out and in separate corners of the room. I looked at my chest, and to my surprise I could not see any sign of marks or injury.

I never told my family what happened because it is best that they don't know, and to be honest they would be really disappointed in me. I still carry the same Bible with me, though, and my faith in God is stronger than ever. I spent all the next day praying in each room of the house, to bless it and protect it.

OLD CLOCK – VILLAGE STREET, DERBY

My parents live a really old house near to Village Street in Derby. One day their neighbour told them about a strange old man who had lived in the house with his family before them. He had an old clock in his living room that never worked.

According to the neighbour, when the man got old and died his wife decided to have his coffin at home for the night prior to the funeral. He was placed in the living room beside the clock. His family and friends came to the house to pay their last respects, and as they stood around his coffin they all heard a faint noise. Everyone turned around to see what it was and to their surprise found that what they could hear was ticking coming from the broken clock.

The really strange thing is that no matter what type of clock my parents have in the house, it always stops working within a matter of days.

SOMEONE'S IN THE MIRROR – DERBY

When I was 12 years old, right up the street from my house in Derby was a large, four-storey, old brick building that has served many purposes over the years. At the time it was an antiques shop; lamps and lights in the basement, big furniture on the first floor, smaller items on the third and nothing but mirrors on the fourth.

One day I stopped in to ask about a part-time job, and much to my surprise I was hired and made a really good amount of money per hour. I loved antiques, and at the time I felt really great making my own money.

However, I soon began to sense that there was something eerie about the building, and strange things started to happen. Sometimes the air in the cellar would go icy cold and the air would follow me around, and there would always be a horrible stench as though something was rotten. I would only stay down there long enough to get what I had to do done. I often got the feeling I was being watched in the basement, but the worst experiences I had were on the fourth floor and in the attic.

The attic was big and full of mirrors, and when I was dusting the mirrors one day the air temperature suddenly dropped about 50 degrees. I felt nauseated and put my hand to my mouth because I thought I was going to be sick. Then in the mirror which was lying lengthwise on the floor next to me I saw a ghostly pair of legs and the butt of an old rifle, seemingly standing to attention right next to me.

I could see that the trousers were blue with red stripes down them and had white leggings covering the lower legs. Suddenly, the legs in the mirror turned towards me and the butt of the rifle slammed down on the floor, on my foot! Terrified, I must have broken every speed record as I ran down four flights of stairs and out the building.

I was dripping with sweat and felt really sick. I never went back to the shop after that day, not even for my last pay check. The owner had to bring it to my house. To this day I do not like mirrors and sometimes wonder if an old mirror acts as a portal to that 'other world'.

MY POSSESSED AUNT – DERBY

I used to live in a suburb of Derby in a large house, with my mum, aunt and grandmother. Our life was perfect, except for one thing – our next door neighbours were awful. My grandmother never told us why the lady next door hated her so much.

One day my aunt, who wasn't much older than me as my grandmother had had her late in life, came home from school very hungry. The lady next door was outside on the porch, and she asked my aunt to help her get something out of the house because it was too heavy to carry alone. As my aunt proceeded to help I tried to stop her, but just as I did so I felt like I was pushed by an unseen force. I did not see anybody by the door at the time. I ran to my grandmother to let her know what was going on, but it was too late!

We ran next door to check on my aunt, but as we approached the door she was already coming out and she had a sandwich in her hand. My grandmother took it away from her but she had almost eaten it all.

That night, at around midnight, I was woken by the smell of something burning. I woke everybody up to help find where the smell was coming from, and it was coming from my aunt's room. I frantically tried the handle but couldn't open the door, and then my grandma tried. Eventually she managed to open the door and made her way inside, but suddenly she stopped in her tracks. The look on her face was as if she had seen the devil himself. I grabbed her hand and she snapped out of her trance. I turned to see who or what she was staring at, and what I saw was the scariest thing I had ever seen. My aunt was sitting in her bed, bolt upright, staring at me. Her face was contorted as if a demon inside her was trying to come out.

She became worse over the next few days. It started with her passing out and then writhing on the floor as though some evil entity inside of her was trying to leave her body. As she writhed her voice changed, and we heard horrible demonic voices of a little girl and a man intermingled with her own. There was even one terrifying time when she began to say that she was possessed by the devil himself. I was so scared to be alone with her, but every time she passed out she seemed to be next to me. The little girl's spirit tried to come through every time I was in front of her. On one occasion I was walking past my aunt, unaware that she was having an episode of possession, when all of a sudden she grabbed me. Her face was not hers and I screamed so hard I almost passed out.

After a few days my grandmother called the local priest and he arrived in minutes. Just as she got off the telephone my aunt, or rather the demon working through her, grabbed me again, pulled me closer and told me that she knew who I was and to watch myself, because one day I would not be so lucky. He came to bless our house but only made it to our door, saying, 'I cannot come in there. It is too strong for me. I need more people with me.'

He told my grandmother that one of the entities was not a mere demon but was the devil himself. When I overheard this I was too shocked to speak, as my aunt had been saying all along that she was possessed by the devil. The priest said that as he was leaving he heard the entity scream at him, saying that her soul was offered to him.

He was so concerned that he came back the very next day with three other priests. They entered the house alone while we gathered outside. I do not know what rituals they performed in there, but whatever it was they did they failed and my aunt remained the same. Days turned into weeks, weeks into months and months into years. Yes, this went on for two years.

I still don't know how she was cured. None of my family members would tell me how. I still feel as if the demon that threatened me is still with her and I am cautious of her.

THE LAUGHING GIRL – DERBY

My mother was once given a picture of a girl by one of her friends. It was not the most attractive picture, but as it was a gift my mother felt it would be rude not to keep it. Several years later she remarried and moved to

Derby, and the man she married made it clear that he did not want the picture of the girl in the new house as it had always given him the creeps, so my mother gave it to me and I kept it in my living room.

A few months ago my boyfriend was tired and went to bed, so I was alone in the living room I went into the kitchen and ran the tap to get a drink of water, then I heard and felt someone behind me. Thinking it was my boyfriend, I turned around and said, 'Okay, what?' but no one was there.

I walked out of the kitchen, a little disturbed, and I heard what sounded like a girl's laugh. I span around and said, 'Hello? Who's there?' No one said anything, and everyone was asleep. I took two more steps and once again heard the laughing. When I turned again my eyes were drawn to the picture of the little girl, as the laughter seemed to be coming from it. I leaned forward to look at the picture, which was not hung on the wall yet, and as I did so it fell forward towards me. I dropped the glass of water in terror, ran out of the living room and upstairs to where my boyfriend was sleeping. As I lay under the duvet I heard footsteps by my door and laughter for about 20 minutes after that.

The next day I took the picture to the tip as there was no way that I was having it in the house as there was something very strange and wrong with it.

MARILYN - ILKESTON

My name is Mike. I am 30 years old and live in Ilkeston. About four years ago I ordered a sign with Marilyn Monroe's picture on it from the internet. When I finally got it and put it up it looked great.

One night I was in my room trying to get to sleep as it was really late, and I was so comfy in my bed that I could not be bothered to get up and switch the light off. I eventually drifted off to sleep, then all of a sudden I woke with a strange, horrible feeling that someone were standing there, looking at me. The feeling was terrible.

As I got up there, right beside my bed, was a blonde haired woman, see-through like a ghost, just staring at me. Then, before I could properly register what I saw seeing, she was gone. I lay awake all night and I got to thinking that it might have been Marilyn Monroe. I don't know; but I do know that I was so scared. I took the picture down the next day and it has never been put back up.

POSSESSED BLANKET - DERBY

I am a 12-year-old girl and I very strongly believe in ghosts and spirits. About three months ago, when I was very tired and just recovered from flu I lay down to take a rest. A few hours later I woke up to a strange noise, but I thought it was just a dream and went back to sleep. Shortly after my mother came in to wake me up because I had been sleeping for quite a long time.

When I was ready to get up, I threw the blanket off me into the middle of the bed and stood up, but as I walked out of the room I heard something behind me, and it sounded like someone moving. I turned around, and the blanket from my bed was right there behind me. I thought nothing of it, assuming that it had got caught by my foot when I left the bed, but it started to move! I froze, and as I reached forwards to pick it up I was really hoping the dog was under it. I picked it up and threw it across the room, but the dog was not there. Then, to my surprise, the blanket started to move again. Scared out of my mind, I ran across the hall and down the stairs. I told my mum what had happened, and we went up to my room together. When we entered we were shocked to see that my bed was made! My mum thought that I had dreamt the whole thing, and now my family thinks I am insane!

SLEEP PARALYSIS - DERBY

One morning I awoke and looked at my alarm clock, but as I tried to roll over I found that I could not move or speak. All I could do was move my eyes and look around me. I was terrified and tried to tell myself that I was dreaming. However, I looked above me at the ceiling and saw a black shadowy figure. I had no idea what it was, but I then began to sense that it wanted to hurt me.

To my horror, I found that I still could not move as it started to come closer to me, and it stopped at the left side of my head. Whatever it was started to make a soft humming noise in my left ear. After that it slowly faded away.

Just when I thought the shadowy figure was gone, it suddenly appeared again on the other side of my room, only it was much bigger this time. It stopped in the middle of my room and made a loud screaming noise. It was very strange, and scary, and sounded like more than one person screaming.

I so badly wanted to scream for my brother in the next room, but nothing would come out. Right after that I found that I could not breathe, as if I was being choked. As the pressure on my throat built up to the point where I felt I could no longer take it, suddenly the figure faded away and I was able to move again.

I later told my brother what had happened and he seemed to think that I was crazy. After seeing a psychologist, she told me that I was not crazy and what happened to me was called sleep paralysis. It has not happened to me again, however, and I hope it never does.

MY LITTLE GUARDIAN ANGEL - ETWALL

About 10 years ago, when I was about 12 years old, I remember I was in my room at my home in Etwall and I heard someone calling my name. It sounded like a little girl's voice, but I still went and asked my parents if they had called me. They said not so I went back to my room and brushed it off as nothing.

Then about 10 minutes later I heard the voice again. It was definitely a little girl's voice. She called my name in a playful way. At first I heard her in one corner of the room, then another. I did not hear her again for a couple days, until I was in school and was in the library, then I heard her almost every day after that, and it continued for a couple of months.

One night I was in my room and I heard her again. She called my name and began to laugh. I was feeling brave so I asked her what she wanted, but she carried on laughing. I turned around and began to walk off, but just as I was leaving I heard the bouncing of a ball behind me. I turned and saw a small ball bouncing up and down all by itself.

As I watched the ball, it began to bounce towards me. I grabbed it and threw it back. All of a sudden it stopped bouncing in midair, then it dropped on the floor and began to bounce again. I was very frightened by this point, but I was transfixed by the sight in front of me, until it stopped bouncing as if someone's hand was over it.

She began laughing again, and that is when thing got too scary and I left. I told my parents about what had happened, but they did not believe me, so I decided to tell my dad's best friend, who is a psychic. She told me that the girl was my guardian angel and she was watching over me.

After the encounter with the ball, I never heard from the girl again. I don't know why she was calling my name, but if I ever hear a little girl's voice calling me from now on, I will know not to be scared.

DARK STRANGER - DERBY

One night at about 3.00am I was lying in bed and my vision was dark and fuzzy. For some reason I could not shake the feeling that something was terribly wrong, and I sensed an evil force lurking in my bedroom. Suddenly I realised that I could not move, nor could I scream as I was paralysed.

I began to panic, when I suddenly saw a black fuzzy figure move through my doorway. I closed my eyes, hoping I was just seeing things, but when I opened them it was standing beside me, leaning right over me. All I could see were two white misty circles that I thought were its eyes. I felt weaker than I had ever felt, and eventually I passed out.

This terrifying ordeal happened on and off for weeks.

THE THING - DERBY

A little while ago my girlfriend and I were staying at a hotel in Derby and as I was out of work at the time I speculatively asked if they had any jobs available. I was in luck, and about a week later I started work there.

It was my first night on reception, and my girlfriend and I were going to stay at the hotel that night because we couldn't move into our new flat until the following day. As I was settling myself in at the reception desk a man came into the hotel. He was wearing a long black coat and a large hat. I smiled at him and said, in my best receptionist voice, 'I am sorry we are full.' To my surprise he got really mad and walked out the door. After a short while I went to close up, and all of a sudden the doors just slammed shut.

I looked out the door and to my horror I could see the man from earlier staring at me with a pair of horrible red eyes. They seemed to get really close, and I could see they looked full of malice and evil. The man then opened his mouth to show me his big, long, sharp teeth.

I have no idea what it was but it was not from this world.

FROZEN WITH FEAR - HARRINGTON STREET, DERBY

We used to live in Harrington Street in Derby, and one night I awoke to the sound of my mum and her friend talking outside my room and saying goodbye to each other as my mum's friend was leaving after a short visit. I was lying on my left side and suddenly a strange feeling came over my body, it was like I was paralysed.

As I lay there I felt a body kneel down onto my bed. I had a water bed and it moved as the person knelt down. And although I could not move at all I could definitely feel this person staring at me really closely.

I tried to call out to my mum but no sound would come out of my mouth. I managed to cry help two or three times, but it was not loud enough for anyone to hear. When my mum's friend left and she walked back into the house, the body got up (and once again I felt the bed move) and instantly I could move again. I rolled over as fast as I could and looked around me, still in shock, but there was nobody there.

The next day I told my parents what had happened, and once we had ruled out sleep paralysis my dad told me that something similar had happened to him while he was living in Scotland.

He told me that he was living with two roommates, while his mother and the rest of his family were living in Newcastle. He was disturbed during his sleep and awoken by his bedroom door slamming. He then heard his mother's voice saying, 'Come on. Get out of bed. Come and eat breakfast,' while his cupboards were opening and closing as if she was putting clothes away or something. He was frozen with fear because he knew his mother was several hundred miles away, and he could not move his body while all of this was happening. Then he heard his bedroom door slam again and he was fine after that. As soon as he was able, he ran out to his two roommates, who were playing cards in another room, and he asked them if any of them had been into his room. Neither of them had.

I do not know exactly what this experience means, or if it is even 'ghostly', but it sure scared the hell out of me.

I have been even more scared since a friend of mine claims to have seen a ghostly figure of an old man sitting behind my chair in the lounge a little while ago.

THE SADNESS - CHADDESDEN

Just a few months ago I was asked to join a few friends who were going to a cemetery as they had a keen interest in both history and the paranormal. We all arrived at Derby Road cemetery in Chaddesden filled with anticipation, and to be honest a touch of trepidation.

We parked the car, and for some reason I had an instant chill that I could not shake, and I knew that something was not as it should be.

We all stepped out of the car and started to approach the gates. All of a sudden I started to feel very heavy, and the closer I got to those gates, the heavier I felt.

Slowly we all entered the cemetery, not saying a word to each other, and I could feel an overwhelming sadness. The further into the cemetery I walked, the sadder I became, but before entering I had been perfectly happy.

After a few minutes I went in a separate direction to my friends, and I found myself standing under a large tree with a group of headstones under it, which were so old that the writing on them was no longer legible. I started to sob uncontrollably, and I felt as if my heart were breaking, but I had no reason to be sad and it was completely out of character as I don't easily cry at things. I felt uncomfortable, so I started to walk back to catch up with my friends.

As I turned to walk away I heard what sounded like another sob, but this time not my own. There, from the corner of my eye, I glimpsed what looked like a figure huddled up underneath the old tree. Before I could blink it was gone.

At that I started to run back to my friends, who had already made it back to the gates. By the time we made it to the car I felt a little better and had stopped sobbing. My friends were totally amazed when I told them what had happened as they had not witnessed anything in the cemetery that day.

Angel of Halloween - Spondon

On Halloween in 1996, my friends and I had at least three bags full of sweets from trick-or-treating around Spondon, so we decided to go home for the night because it was getting late and we had school the next morning.

When we got home my brother and I sat in the living room until Aaron went to find our mother, who was in the other room. I sat down on the sofa and started to dig through my trick-or-treat bag, looking for some chocolate. Suddenly, from nowhere, I saw a female figure standing by the front door, and I could see that her hair was curly and dark brown and she was dressed in a white robe and looked exactly like my mother, except for the fact that she had a golden glow around her head. I stared at her but then I started to freak out and ran into my mother's bedroom. My brother was already in there, eating his sweets totally oblivious to the weird angel or ghost that I had seen.

I told my mother what the figure looked like, describing her in all the detail I could, and when I mentioned the golden glow she was sure that it must have been an angel.

LITTLE BOY WANTS TO PLAY? – DERBY

This is a story my granny told me, and it happened to her a long time ago when she was a little girl living on Curzon Street in Derby. One day she was ill and had to go to hospital, where she stayed for three days. On the third day she saw a little boy by her bedside with yellow glowing hair and dressed all in white. He was jumping and playing all about her.

She screamed for the nurse to get the little boy away, but when the nurse came to help her she said, 'There is no one near you.'

My granny looked up, puzzled, then noticed that the little boy had disappeared. She is sure, to this day, that a ghost came to her – maybe it was a boy who had died in the hospital.

ST FRANCIS OF ASSISI – DUFFIELD

I have always been religious and had attended St Mary's Church in Derby for many years before I moved to Duffield. St Francis of Assisi is the patron saint of all animals, and there have been occasions when that I have said desperate prayers to him for my pets. I now have two small dogs, and one of them lost the use of his hind legs and was in a lot of pain. I took him to the vet and he suggested that I had him put to sleep. The dog was in a lot of pain because a bone in his back had dislodged itself, crippling him and putting painful pressure on his spine. I refused, however, and begged the vet to do whatever he could to try and help him.

That night I again prayed to St Francis, begging him to make my dog better as I could not bear to lose him. After four days I got a phone call from the vet, but it was not my regular vet who called. He asked me to come and see him about my dog, so I went even though I had never met the vet before. I arrived at the surgery expecting the worst.

I discovered that my usual vet was not there, and instead found a young vet who was tall, with dark curly hair and big, brown, gentle eyes. He informed me that the dog's pain was easing. He then told me to take my dog home and have patience and faith. So, I took him home and let him into the backyard, which was always one of his favourite play spots. At first my little dog looked at me with sorrow in his eyes, then, incredibly, his back leg started to twitch.

The next day he was up and running on three legs and the day after he was on four. He completely recovered. When I rang my vet and told him about his recovery, all he could say was that it was a miracle. I asked about the vet who had been so kind, and was told that he had left the surgery. From what I have been told, he has travelled to Asia to try and rescue some of the abused cats and dogs there.

TRUE LOVE – SHARDLOW

A couple of years ago I was asleep in my bed in Shardlow and I had a dream that I was in a graveyard walking up to a headstone. When I got there I read a female name, and the dates were 1987–2006. Then, all of a sudden, a young woman appeared. She had black hair and a pale face and wore a white sweater with jeans.

'Hi Dan. We were supposed to fall in love,' she said, but she did not move her lips. With tears in her eyes, she gave me a sweet, soft smile. I awoke right then and stayed up all night. It felt so real because the dream had so much substance and emotion to it.

A couple of days later I actually cried thinking about her, and I could not shake the dream girl from my head, so I decided to do some research on the internet to see if she actually ever existed. Given the realistic nature of the dream, I was not at all surprised when I saw a photograph of her on the screen in which she was wearing the same sweater and jeans she had worn when she had visited me in my sleep.

I know that people can read things and store the information in their subconscious, but I truly cannot remember ever reading about this girl, and I did not live in Derby at the time. Also, the emotions that I felt that night were very raw, and I am therefore convinced that I was visited by a girl that I had been destined to be with.

THE HOODED THING - UTTOXETER NEW ROAD, DERBY

In December 1983 I decided to walk home from school through the graveyard on Uttoxeter New Road as it was the quickest way back to my house. When I was about halfway through the entrance gate it suddenly slammed shut and pushed me forward. Then I felt cold inside, as if something went straight through me. I had walked through the graveyard many times as my grandparents were buried there, but I had never experienced anything like this before.

As I carried on walking I looked behind me to see if I could see anything wrong with the gate, and right there was a strange figure in a black hood. As I turned to look a whatever it was, it pulled something out of its pocket. My first reaction was to run, but my legs wouldn't move. The thing started to walk closer to me, and I was really panicking. It seemed to be shimmering and was hovering about 2ft above the ground. I could see through it in certain places but it was solid in others. The scariest thing was that I could not see a face, although looking back it was probably a good thing as I am sure the image would have haunted me for the rest of my life.

WHO ATTACKED GRANDMA? - CHADDESDEN

One fine summer evening my grandma and I were visiting my grandad's grave in Chaddesden. My grandma likes to talk to his grave, so I left her to it for an hour while I took a walk.

When I came back I was shocked to find my grandma lying on the ground, convulsing as if someone were strangling her. I ran to help her, but there was nothing I could do and I couldn't get her up. I started to panic and quickly grabbed her, and suddenly she stopped struggling. She fell unconscious in my arms, and then I had an overwhelming sense that my grandad missed her and wanted her to join him in death. No sooner had I felt this, my grandmother opened her eyes and said that she had seen grandad and he was at peace.

Although the experience was really frightening at the time, I am actually glad that it happened because it helped my grandmother believe that death does not mean the end. My grandmother passed away shortly after this and the family felt great comfort knowing that they are now together again.

'I SEE YOU' – DERBY

I was Goth in the early 1990s, and whenever I had free time I would read at various cemeteries in Derby as I always found them havens of peace and quiet. One morning I was sitting in a cemetery reading and from nowhere I heard the words, 'I see you.'

At first I thought it was just someone having a joke with me, so I rolled my eyes and thought no more of it. After a few seconds, however, I heard my phone ring, and when I answered it I couldn't hear anyone on the other end. Then all of a sudden I heard the words, 'I see you,' again, but this time they were being spoken through my phone.

I was absolutely petrified and looked around me but saw nobody else. I was so scared that I never read in cemeteries again or wore my Goth clothing, as I was sure that it had attracted something of a paranormal nature. I am not sure if it is just a coincidence, but since I decided to dress differently I have not heard or seen anything paranormal.

THE DAY TIME STOOD STILL – DERBY

One day I was in my kitchen cooking tea and I happened to glance at the kitchen clock, which said 5.10pm, and I made a mental note of what time the tea would be cooked. I then went into the conservatory and started to read the newspaper. After a little while I glanced down at my watch and it said also said 5.10pm and I convinced myself that the clock in the kitchen must be fast as at least five minutes had passed since I looked at it. I continued to read for what seemed like half an hour, then I checked my watch again, and it still said 5.10pm. I thought the battery must have stopped so I checked the watch more closely, and to my astonishment I saw the second hand was ticking around as normal. More than a little confused, I walked back into the kitchen to check on the food and saw that the kitchen clock still said 5.10pm.

By now I was totally confused so I went into the lounge to put the television on teletext so I could see the correct time. I was absolutely astounded to see that the television was also showing that the time was 5.10pm.

I went back into the kitchen and checked on the food in the oven and it was nearly ready, proving to me that it had been cooking for at least 40 minutes, yet all the clocks in the house only said 5.11pm. I have no idea what happened, but it would seem that my world froze at 5.10pm on that day.

RUN LIKE THE CLAPPERS! – DERBY

This is not my story, it is my friend's parents' friend's, if that makes any sense at all. Their friend, named John, and his friends grew up in Derby in the 1940s and always used to go to a local cemetery at night and play pranks on each other when they were children.

One particular night they went out to a cemetery as usual, and it was a very foggy, misty night. As they were exploring in the gloom, they came across a large gothic tombstone with a huge bell over it. When they inspected the grave more closely they saw a rope attached to the bell. Then suddenly the bell started to ring.

The group of children were all scared now, but John, the bravest, walked over to the grave to see what was causing the bell to ring. He noticed, to his horror, that there was no clapper inside to make it ring and that nobody was holding the end of the rope. Somehow the bell was ringing itself. At this revelation, they screamed, ran away and vowed never to return to the graveyard.

BATH TIME – PEAK DISTRICT

In the early 1960s a friend and her partner bought a house in a small village in the Peak District, in a very rural area with no power or hot water. The house obviously had not been lived in for many years, and they purchased it with the intention to renovate it.

A little way away from their house was an overgrown field which was part of their land, and on it was a shed. Next to the shed there was an old bathtub and a mirror. My friend assumed that they had once belonged in the house but had been dumped there after a previous renovation.

After my friend had been living in the house for a little while she took me down to see the field, and as soon as I saw the bath in her field I began to get a strange feeling in my stomach. My chest suddenly felt tight as if I was having an asthma attack, and I had not suffered with it since I was very small. I looked over at the bath and I could see blood and a fair-haired woman crying over it.

Terrified by the images that had flashed into my head, I told my friend I had to leave and we went back to her house, where she made me a hot, sweet cup of tea for the shock. I told her what had happened and she told me that many of her friends had felt the same feeling and that one other had even seen the same shocking image as me.

We asked an old lady who had lived in the village all her life about the house and field, and she told us that when she was a child – at the turn of the century – a rumour had gone around the village that a mother of a little girl had suffered post-natal depression and had tried to drown her baby in the bathtub.

Could I have seen the spirit of the mother riddled with guilt for what she was trying to do to her baby daughter?

STANDING FIRM – DERBY

Some people believe that buildings develop a feeling from the souls of the people who have previously lived in them. Our story is one of many similar tales, but this one is about a building that did not want to be demolished.

It was 1970 and there was major refurbishment work being done in and around the city of Derby. The accommodation quarters of our local pub were to be pulled down as the building was beyond economical repair. The accommodation block was constructed of weatherboard with an iron roof, and it had originally been transported there in various sections from different locations and joined together to make one large residence at the turn of the last century. The publican lived in one end of these quarters.

My husband and I were allowed to pull the building down ourselves so we could use the materials instead of it merely being bulldozed and burnt. But right from the first day odd things happened, which were at first put down to the state of the building. Then such things as tools being placed next to you that were then found in other rooms. Eventually a specific room or spot was designated to keep everything in but things were still moved around. This was put down to carelessness initially, until major things started to happen, some of which were potentially life threatening.

The first such incident occurred when my husband was up in the roof to get the roofing iron off. He was standing on the wall structure, when suddenly two ceilings and the structure completely collapsed under him, leaving him hanging from the roof trusses. My husband had checked the structure for stability prior to the work being started as some sections of the building were not safe enough to do this, and so he was very shocked.

As we got further into the building more and more inexplicable events happened and we were all beginning to feel unnerved. We heard hammering in rooms where no one was working and footsteps down empty hallways, and my husband also saw dark shapes and shadows pass him go past him into other rooms. This mostly happened towards the end of the demolition, almost as though they were upset about what was going on.

My husband's brother also came to help and experienced events, such as talking to what he thought was my husband standing behind him while he worked only to find that he had not been anywhere near him. This often happened to both men. My brother-in-law took his ladder into one of the rooms that had given particular resistance to being pulled down to start centre-punching the timber lining boards for removal, when suddenly a lining board directly above him sprang loose and hit him on the head. The funny thing about this board was that it took both men to pull it down and the rest of the ceiling was more resistance to being pulled down than the rest of the building.

Some people may say that spirits cannot hurt you, but during the last days of demolition many small accidents occurred – with the most significant being a direct attack on my husband. He had just come down off the ladder and was standing perfectly still, thinking about what had to be done next, when he said he felt someone kick the side of his knee with such force that it dropped him like a bag of spuds to the floor. We took him to the hospital for treatment, and he was then referred to a specialist and now requires surgery as they do not know what is wrong with it.

In the same end of the building the workmen had managed to remove most of the walls and frames, leaving two walls in each room holding up the roof. The roof could not be removed as mentioned earlier as it was not safe to do so. At this point, every time they approached the building to do further work it would groan and creak in defiance and start to move as though it was trying to fall on them and when they moved away from the building it would stop. As crazy as it sounds, we knew that this last part of the building had to be tricked into submission, so one man stood at the corner of the building and let it do its groaning thing, while another ran around the building with drag chains and hooked it up to the lorry to pull it down.

It took a lot to get this section of the building down, and yet it was the most unstable part. When I asked the publican's wife if anything odd had ever happened in the building in the years they had lived there, she replied that she would call out to her kids to get back to bed late at night as she could hear them walking up and down the hallways and rustling in the kitchen, but found them asleep or in their rooms. She did not reveal much more, but said that the building had its ghosts, and we believe that she was right.

CHAPTER 4

A premonition is a temporary state of mind that usually occurs prior to traumatic events such as accidents or deaths, and it is usually caused by anxiety and unease, which induces an apprehension of a probable future event. It often occurs when in the first stages of sleep as the brain is in transition from alpha to theta waves. This stage is sometimes referred to as somnolence.

DEATH CLOCK – DERBYSHIRE

My Auntie Elizabeth was the oldest sister of my father Fred. She had virtually raised him throughout his childhood as his father had gone to war and then when he returned he worked long hours in the pit.

Auntie Elizabeth lived in a rather grand house in north Derbyshire with her husband, who had worked as a stationmaster. She was a wealthy woman who was known for her sharp tongue and she never missed an opportunity to comment on my appearance or the state of our financial affairs.

To say that I hated visiting my aunt is an understatement, and I often felt that visiting the Queen would be far less stressful. Yet every last Sunday of the month we would make the journey to her house and my parents would read me the riot act about how to behave and to remember my manners.

I can clearly remember one occasion, when I was eight years old, going to visit my aunt because the house seemed very creepy that day for some reason and I can remember being too scared to go to the toilet on my own as the house had such a strange air about it.

We were sitting around the dining table having lunch when the conversation turned on to the subject of my aunt's health. I was not really paying attention to the conversation and instead passed some time by counting the chimes on the old grandfather clock, which stood in the corner of the room. As I counted I realised that the clock had struck 13 times. Totally confused by this, I tried to get my mother's attention but was quickly silenced. My aunt then said, 'I will not be leaving this world without my favourite brother.' The adults all laughed at my aunt's remarks, but her words sent a chill down my back. Throughout my childhood, and indeed my adult years, I never forgot my aunt's words, but rationalised that my aunt was several years older than my father so the likelihood of them dying together was almost impossible.

In 2001 I moved into a new home. On the day of the move my parents came round to help me unpack. My father bent forwards to open a box and suddenly collapsed – he suffered a fatal heart attack. As you can imagine, the next few minutes were total panic as I called the ambulance and frantically tried to resuscitate him. I glanced at the clock as I tried to time my CPR and it was three o'clock.

The rest of the day passed in a blur as I took my mother back to her house and stayed with her, totally consumed by our grief. I also took on the task of contacting the rest of the family and soon found myself dialling my Auntie Elizabeth to inform her.

The phone rang for a while, and then my uncle answered. I asked to speak to my aunt but my uncle broke down: 'I've been trying to reach your father all day,' he cried, 'Auntie Elizabeth passed away at two o'clock as she took her afternoon nap.'

I put the phone down feeling totally shaken as my aunt's words from that childhood visit came back to haunt me. She was true to her word and did not leave this world without her favourite brother, dying just an hour before him.

BLACK AND WHITE – DERBY

I was born in the 1940s near Vernon Street in Derby and lived in a beautiful house there with my mother and three siblings. My eldest sister, Edna, lived nearby in Wolfa Street, and as she worked, my mother would often look after her twin boys, John and James. My mother adored the boys because she had only been blessed with girls. She relished knitting and dressing them in matching pram sets and would proudly push their big, coach-built pram up and down Friargate, knowing that she would be stopped several times by women wanting to admire the children.

One day I came home from school to find that the boys were at our home, but it was not on a day that my sister was working.

'Your sister isn't feeling very well today, so I said that I would have the boys for her while she rested,' my mother explained.

The boys were sitting in the middle of the best room floor, playing with some chalk and a slate board that used to belong to me when I was a child. I reached over to see what scribbles the boys had done but nothing could have prepared me for what I saw. There, in big white letters on the slate board, were the words HOME NOW.

I asked the boys if they had done it, but they were too young to even understand my question let alone write and spell correctly. Puzzled, I ran to my mother and asked her if she knew anything about the words. She stopped what she was doing and turned to have a look herself.

'I didn't write this, but it must be a warning about Edna' she said as she suddenly dashed out of the back door. I returned to the boys and we sat playing for what seemed like hours, waiting for my mother to return.

Later that evening my mother arrived home and told me that on arriving at Edna's house she found the back door slightly open, which was not like Edna as she was very safety conscious. She had then gone upstairs and found Edna thrashing about on the bed having some type of fit, so my mother ran to fetch the doctor.

Thankfully, my sister made a full recovery and never had a fit again. My mother was sure that the message on the slate was written by my sister's guardian angel as there was no way that anyone else could have written the message at such a crucial time.

NIGHTMARE SAVES THE DAY – ALVASTON

One night in October 1998 I had the worst night's sleep imaginable. Tossing and turning all night, I finally went to sleep at around 3am and had a terrible nightmare, which was so bad that I woke up again at 3.30am and lay awake for the rest of the night.

The nightmare seemed so real. It involved my family and I travelling to Bardills garden centre. We were travelling along the A52 and I clearly saw a man roll down the embankment, and then he lay dead just inches from the main carriageway. All the cars were racing past and nobody stopped to help, and I can remember feeling sad in my nightmare that this was someone's son and nobody came to help.

I could not shake the image of the young man from my mind, and I can tell you I was more than relieved when the rest of the family awoke. When my husband came downstairs he announced that he wanted to go to Bardills that morning to get a few bits and bobs for the garden. This was a major coincidence as it certainly was not the nearest garden centre to us in Alvaston and he had never mentioned it before. I told him all about my nightmare and asked if we could go to another garden centre, but his mind was made up so I soon found myself heading down the A52.

We arrived safely and had a pleasant time looking at all the plants, although my husband took the opportunity to mock me for my foolishness in thinking that my nightmare was real.

After returning to the car we set off for home. We had travelled no further than 200 yards when I saw a strange bundle lying near the side of the road. The hairs stood up on the back of the neck as I screamed at my husband that there was a body lying at the side of the road, and I begged him to turn the car around. The nearest turning point was at the Long Eaton junction and my husband did nothing but moan as he turned the car around and headed back towards Bardills.

As we approached the same spot my husband slowed the car right down and I pointed out the odd bundle lying there at the side of the road. He pulled over onto the hard shoulder and I told him I was getting out. As I approached the bundle I could see it was a man, and he was unconscious. I knelt beside him and felt for a pulse as I dialled the emergency services for assistance.

Within a matter of minutes the police and ambulance arrived and took over, so after giving my details we returned to the car and went home.

Thankfully the man was not dead, he was unconscious from a suspected drug overdose. I strongly believe that my nightmare was a warning and that without it nobody would have stopped to help the man, and he could have died.

Satan snake - Nottingham

I have always been into pets, especially snakes, and I pestered my mum until she agreed to buy me one for my 14th birthday. After having the snake for a few months, it escaped from the tank and went missing for a month or two, but we finally found it slithering up the staircase – I was so relieved. At last the family started to visit again!

I eventually sold the snake to my mate Andy as my parents no longer wanted it in the house in case it escaped again. I did miss it at first, but I knew that I could always get another one when I was older.

Eight years passed and I moved into rented accommodation with a few of my friends. After a few months I asked the landlord if he minded me having a pet snake in the house, and he was fine with it, so on payday I bought myself a little baby corn snake. Corn snakes are the tamest you can buy, so I thought everything would be fine. I purchased the snake and excitedly took it back home.

The snake was the tamest pet I had ever had. Then in July 2003 something totally unexplainable happened. During the night I had a terrible nightmare that my corn snake had escaped from the tank and I saw an evil spirit enter its body. Then the snake started attacking my family by biting us. I woke up in a cold sweat, but after I calmed down I thought nothing more about it because, after all, dreams are just dreams – right?

The following morning I went over to my snake and picked it up, when suddenly it attacked me. The snake's mouth was attached to one of my fingers and my nightmare had come true. I managed to get the snake off my finger and slammed the lid back on the tank, but the snake carried on attacking the tank, trying to bite me and head-butting the glass in the process. It did this constantly for the next few days.

After a week the snake was still behaving aggressively so I decided to take it back to the pet shop. When I explained to the shop assistant what had happened, he looked at me like I was from a different planet as he explained that it was very unusual behaviour for a corn snake.

I couldn't believe what I then witnessed. The shopkeeper picked up the snake and it was as tame as when I first got it. He gave me my money back and clearly thought that I had gone crazy. There are two things I am sure about: one is that somehow my nightmare passed over some kind of evil spirit to my snake and the other is that I will never own another one for as long as I live.

FINAL GOODBYE – SHARDLOW

My dad's aunt was an elderly lady, and despite the vast age difference I had become increasingly close to her throughout my adult years. I would pop in to visit her at her home in Ripley, and I spent many afternoons sitting and listening to her stories about her life.

My great aunt's life always fascinated me and she had certainly lived it to the full, dedicating it to working with children as a teacher and a leader in the Girl Guides. Although she had surrounded herself with children, she had never married and never had children of her own.

My father was her favourite nephew and she loved to tell me stories about his childhood and how she had played a part in bringing him up. She adored him, my brother, sister and me equally. In fact I always considered her to be more like a grandmother than a great aunt.

She lived in Ripley all her life and as her health started to fail it became apparent that she needed to go into a nursing home, so she was moved first to a home in Ripley and then to one in Borrowash, so she could be near the rest of the family.

Although she seemed happy in the nursing home and the staff were very good to her, she loved to see members of her own family and would positively light up when I visited her with my children.

When her health deteriorated further she was transferred to a hospital in Shardlow where she could get the health care she needed, and I can remember waking up one morning with an overwhelming urge to go and visit her. All through the day, as I tried to get on with my job, I had the strangest urge to visit and soon realised that I was not going to get any work done until I had seen her.

When I arrived at Shardlow, to my amazement I saw what I am sure was a beautiful angel hovering above the main entrance. It was glowing white and gold.

My great aunt was lying in her hospital bed when I got to the ward and there was definitely something different about her. She did not smile when she saw me and just lay there looking straight into my eyes. Incredibly, when I asked her a question or made conversation her answers appeared in my head but her mouth never moved. It was the strangest conversation I have ever experienced.

Soon it was time for me to go and I leant over and kissed her on her forehead, somehow knowing that this would be the last time I would see her alive. As I walked away down the corridor I heard my great aunt's voice in my head saying, 'I love you.' It was so loud that it stopped me in my tracks and I realised that I had never told my aunt that I loved her too, so I ran back down the corridor as fast as I could, held my aunt's hand and told her as a tear ran down my cheek. My aunt smiled and I knew then that it was our goodbye.

Several days later my aunt was transferred to Derby City Hospital and my parents called me to say that it would not be long before she died. All the family went to hospital to see her but I did not want to go. I felt that we had said our goodbyes in private and thankfully my parents understood.

I lay in bed that night and felt an amazing sense of peace, and I soon fell fast asleep. At around 1am I heard my name being whispered and I opened my eyes to find my bedroom had changed to the hospital ward and I could see my aunt lying in her bed, next to an observation window. Then a small, white-haired lady stood next to my aunt and I watched as she took her last breath. I saw her spirit being lifted from her physical body and floating upwards and also heard the sound of the most beautiful music.

CHILLING TALES FROM DERBYSHIRE

On realising that I was not asleep and that my aunt had passed, I glanced at my clock and wrote down the time. The room then returned to normal, the ward disappeared, and as I sat upright in my bed I didn't know if I should phone my parents to tell them what had happened. I figured that they would both be asleep so I decided to call them in the morning.

My father phoned me at 7am and on answering he said, 'I have some sad news.' Before he had time to finish, I told him I already knew that our aunt had passed and told him what had happened in the night. Incredibly, she had died at exactly the same time that I had written on the note pad at the side of the bed.

SEEING IS BELIEVING – DERBY

One night, as I drifted into the state of unconsciousness, my bedroom suddenly started to fill with a white mist. Rubbing my eyes to get a better view, I could see an aeroplane flying dangerously low and then crashing into an embankment, and below it I could see cars travelling at speed, so I knew that it was flying over a motorway.

Shocked by what I had seen I quickly telephoned my mother, who was more into spiritual things than me, to tell her about my vision. The image before me was very vivid and I could even smell burning engine oil. As I told my mother, the image and the strange mist simply vanished, as quickly as they came. My mother told me to pray and try and get some sleep.

The next day, as I was getting ready for my nine o'clock shift at work, my mother telephoned me and asked if I had seen the news, to which I replied that I hadn't.

'Put the radio on,' she wailed, her voice fearful. 'There has been a plane crash in Kegworth and it happened exactly as you said.'

The only other time I have experienced the mist and visions was just before the twin towers came down. I don't know why I was chosen to see these things when it is clearly obvious that I have no power to change them.

NAME TO REMEMBER – DERBY

I grew up on Abbey Street, Derby, along with my parents and seven brothers and sisters, so money was very tight. As the youngest I was destined to a life of hand-me-down clothes and toys which were all well past their best before I had my hands on them.

To pass the time I would sit and make paper dolls with my sister Anna and would spend hours making up adventures with those scrappy bits of paper – a far cry from what children have now. My favourite paper doll was a male doll, which I had coloured in to show blue trousers and a red sweater. I named him Roy, which looking back was an odd choice as it was not a popular name in the 1950s and I didn't know anybody with the same name. I cherished Roy and played with him all the time, and on many occasions my father would have to mend him with tape, like, for example, when his leg got accidentally torn off!

One day, when I was playing with Roy in the back yard and I had a strange urge to change the doll's name, I ran inside to inform everyone that from now on Roy was to be called Alan. From that day on Alan came with me everywhere, but I could not explain to my parents where the sudden urge to change his name had come from.

Many years later, when I was in my teens, I attended a tea dance and a smart looking man asked me for a dance. He introduced himself as Alan. Without thinking I blurted out that that was the name of my favourite doll when I was a young girl and that I had changed its name to Alan after calling it Roy for many years. I immediately regretted my nervous babble as my new dance partner went silent and looked like he was in shock.

However, the reason for the look on his face soon became apparent. He sat me down and explained that he had been christened Roy as a baby after a soldier his father had met during the war but he had hated it and had later changed it to Alan, his mother's maiden name. We were both stunned further when we worked out that he changed his name at around the same time as I had changed my doll's name.

We soon became inseparable and married a few years later, never spending a day apart from each other in all the time we were married until his death.

So how did I know as a little girl that I needed to change the name of my doll from Roy to Alan? I believe it was fate.

CHAPTER 5

DIVINE INTERVENTION

Divine intervention is when a spiritual or unexplained power has had a hand in changing an outcome, usually giving protection in some way to the person concerned.

A lot of people believe in fate, and in the tales in this chapter it could be argued that although the odds were stacked against the person involved it simply was not their fate or karmic path to proceed in the situation which was being shown, so an outside force changed the outcome.

HOPE – DERBY

I never used to believe in angels and firmly believed that they were nothing more than an imaginary creation by the church in order to keep us mere mortals fearful. Yet what happened to me one night a few years ago changed my life forever.

As you can probably guess, I was never a religious person and totally believed that when one dies that is it – no afterlife, no reincarnation and definitely no heaven.

Leading up to the August night in question, my life seemed to be going from bad to worse. I was in the process of divorcing my husband of 30 years and I had just been made redundant from a job which I loved. My prospects were poor, and although I had an excellent work record (I had been with the same company for 20 years and worked my way up to senior management) there was little chance of me finding a similar company to work for in the Midlands as it was such a specialist field.

Finding myself jobless and alone made me depressed. My life did not seem worth living, and when I looked in the mirror the reflection showed that my once youthful looks had gone and in their place was a washed-out woman. I simply couldn't find any reason for me to live and with each day that passed the yearning to take my own life got stronger and stronger.

One night I decided that tonight would be the night that I took my own life and put an end to my misery, so I sat down and wrote a letter to my daughter who lived in Spain telling her I was sorry and how much I loved her. I know you are probably thinking that I am a selfish woman for wanting to end my life when I had a daughter, but to be honest at that point I truly believed that I was doing her some sort of favour as she wouldn't have to endure the endless tearful telephone calls from me when she was too far away in miles to help me.

As I began to write my farewell letter, I felt the tears flow from my eyes. The tears were splashing on the paper and smudging the words and this concerned me as my daughter would know that I had been crying while I was writing it, but I continued anyhow. I finished it off and sealed it in an envelope then walked the short distance to the post box and put it inside. Then I returned home and collected an assortment of tablets from my medicine cupboard and the bottle of whisky I had been keeping for this event. I then went back into the lounge and sat down clutching my goodies.

Just as I was about to take a handful of pills, I heard a loud voice booming the word no from somewhere behind me.

Knowing that I was alone, I span around in fear and saw what I can only describe as an angel. It was at least 9ft tall and towered above me, with the most brilliant light radiating from it. I would be lying if I said that I saw wings, but somehow I knew that it was an angel rather than a ghost.

'What do you want?' I shouted, rather annoyed that my plan had been interrupted.

'Your life will get better within the week. You must not take your life,' it said. The voice echoed in my head but I could not see its lips moving as its facial features were not visible.

Overcome with emotion, I put the tablets down and thought to myself that as my life had been so terrible I would test the angel's words and give myself one more week to live, then if nothing had changed I would still end my life.

To my surprise, the very next day I received an offer of an interview for a job that I had applied for several months earlier. Apparently the job had become vacant again, so the following Friday I went along to the interview with a lovely man. It went brilliantly and he offered me the job there and then to start the following Monday.

On my very first day in the job my new boss invited me out for lunch and we found that we had a lot in common, so we arranged to go to the theatre the following evening. Not long afterwards we were a couple.

The seventh day arrived and my luck and life had certainly got a lot better, so much had happened in just one week and suddenly I had every reason to live. I was pondering on this when I remembered that I had posted the letter to my daughter and panicked that she must be frantic with worry, so I called her straight away. To my surprise my daughter told me that she had not received any letter from me, and so I didn't tell her of its contents. To this day she has never received it. Was it a coincidence that it had been lost in the post or was it some kind of divine intervention?

EXPECTED DELIVERY DATE – KILBURN

Money was tight as my husband had recently lost his job and I was on maternity leave expecting our first child, so every penny counted.

One Saturday morning and I bent down to collect the mail, which had been posted through our door, only to find that I had a phone bill for £435. This was a huge sum to us and we simply didn't have that kind of money to pay it, so I broke down through worry and probably exhaustion as I had not been sleeping very well due to the size of my growing baby.

Sitting there with tears streaming down my face, I called out the angels for help to find the money to pay the bill, and no sooner had I thought it, I felt an immense sense of calm sweep over me and I knew that the angels had heard me.

The next day my husband and I went to dinner with my parents as we had very little food in the house, and on the way back we called in at a little shop to buy a loaf of bread, a pint of milk and a bar of chocolate. I counted the change and we had £1.90 to our name, which was all the money we had in the world and a very frightening thought.

We continued on our walk along Morley Road and had just passed the entrance to Morley Hayes when I noticed a man begging on the other side of the road. I couldn't understand why he had chosen such a place as the area was not well populated, and as it was a Sunday there was very little passing traffic. He was wearing the most brilliant electric blue anorak and I can remember commenting to my husband that the coat was very clean considering he was a beggar.

Just as we were level with him on the other side of the road I asked my husband to stop the car. He thought I was barmy but pulled over anyway and asked me what I was going to do. I told him that he must go and give the bread, milk, chocolate and the remainder of our money to the beggar. After some protest my husband got out of the car and walked over the road.

'Here you go mate, your need is greater than mine,' my husband said as he handed over the goods.

My husband then turned around and started to walk back towards the car and I noticed that the beggar was following him. I began to panic as I realised that this man could attack us, leaving us stranded in the middle of nowhere.

When he got back to the car, my husband started to wind down the window to see what the man wanted. I felt a growing sense of unease as the man leant his head through the window and looked me straight in the eyes. Despite my nerves, I still had time to notice that I had never seen eyes that were such a brilliant shade of blue. They were crystal clear and almost turquoise in colour.

'God bless you ma'am, your angels are looking after you,' he said to me, which I thought was strange but thanked him anyway.

My husband wound the window back up and the beggar was standing just the other side of the car door, clearly visible through the window. My husband then turned to put his seatbelt on and when he turned back the beggar simply disappeared.

We looked up and down the road but saw nobody and there was no way that in the seconds it took for my husband to put his seat belt on he could have walked out of sight. Both my husband and I sat in silence for the rest of the journey.

The following day I went to fetch the post, and in the bunch of envelopes in my hand I saw that my husband had a letter from the Inland Revenue and so he quickly opened it. He discovered that he had a tax rebate and a cheque for £435 – exactly the same amount as the telephone bill that needed paying.

ANGEL INTERCEPTION – OSMASTON PARK ROAD, DERBY

When I was a small boy I used to ride my bicycle from Sinfin Lane to Osmaston Park Road to visit my grandmother who was bedridden. One lovely summer day my mother asked me to take a parcel to her and so I set off along the road on my rusty bike. I loved my bike and would rarely be seen without it, and despite my young age I was quite an accomplished rider, always paying attention to other road users.

On this particular day I rode past the old army barracks and was waiting at the crossroads to turn right. There was a heavy stream of traffic, so I waited for what seemed like ages with my foot poised on my pedal ready to push off. When it was clear to do so, I went to move forward but strangely my bike would not budge, and try as I might it was fixed to the spot. At the very same time a car sped past right in my path and there is no doubt in my mind that if I had not been prevented from moving forward I would have been hit. As soon as the car had passed I was able to move again.

Shaken by the experience, I decided to walk to my grandmother's house, so I pushed my bike for the rest of the way, carrying the parcel with tears streaming down my cheeks.

When I reached my grandmother's house I let myself in and went straight up to her bedroom to see her, but before I could open the door I heard my grandmother talking to someone and it sounded like she was thanking them.

I knocked on the bedroom door and entered, only to find, to my utter surprise, that my grandmother was alone. She smiled in welcome as I entered, beckoned me closer and hugged me so tight that I thought my eyes would pop out of my head.

'Thank goodness you are safe David,' she said to me. 'I had a dream that you were going to be hit by car that came out of nowhere and I saw you and your bike being tossed into the air. I called in the angels to protect and save you.'

At this I sat down on the bed and told her what had happened to me on my journey to visit her and how my bike had become 'stuck' to the road, preventing me from moving forward. After telling her, I asked her who she had been talking to before I came into the room, and she told me that an angel had appeared to her at the end of the bed and said to her, 'The task is done. He is safe.'

I have spent many hours throughout my life trying to make sense of what happened on that day. Even if my grandmother imagined the angels, I can come up with no reasonable explanation for how she knew that I was so close to becoming involved in a crash or how my bike suddenly stopped working, preventing me moving at that precise time. One thing is for sure, though, if my bike had allowed me to move forward I don't think I would be alive to share this experience with you.

FACE IN THE MIRROR – DERBY

My mum died when I was seven after being involved in a car crash on the M1, so I was raised by my dad and then later on by my stepmother as well when he remarried.

When I left college I worked as a rep for a pharmaceutical company based in Derby, but my role involved driving all over the United Kingdom, which was not a problem to me as I loved driving. I arrived at work one day to be told that I needed to see a company in Leicester, so I picked up my case and walked across to the car. It was a really awful day, the wind and rain was pelting down, and I needed to turn my car lights on as the sky was so dark.

I was just about to reverse out of my parking space when I glanced in my rear-view mirror and saw my mum sitting in the middle of the back seat. I slammed the brakes on in surprise and turned around, but I saw nothing. Thinking that it must have been my imagination, I glanced back in the rear-view mirror again and I could clearly see her again.

I turned the ignition off and started crying as I stared in the mirror transfixed by my mother's beautiful face. Although she did not speak, I had a feeling that she did not want me to go on that journey and no sooner had I thought this she disappeared.

I had to tell my boss that I couldn't go and for fear of seeming silly I told a lie and said that I didn't feel very well and needed to go home. My boss believed my story and even commented that I was as pale as a ghost, so he immediately sent me home.

The next day when I went to work I saw the rep's car, which I had been due to drive the previous day, parked in the car park with its front end all crumpled up.

On entering my workplace I was told that Adrian, one of my colleagues, had been involved in a smash on the M1 when he went to Leicester in my place. He had broken his collarbone but was otherwise unhurt, but looking at the car, Adrian must have had a lucky escape – but not as lucky as I had been, thanks to my mum's warning.

A HELPING HAND - DARLEY PARK

Five years ago my dad passed away. About two weeks after his death, I decided to go for a walk to clear my head and ended up walking past the Broadway pub into Darley Park.

I was walking up the pavement and suddenly a car swerved in the road and lost control. Just as I was about to freeze to the spot I felt someone rugby tackle me, but no one was there.

The car skidded past the very spot that I had been in just a split-second before. I nearly died, and I do not know who or what saved me but I think it was my dad. I have often hoped since then that it was him trying to save my life.

Sunflower Field of Death – St Benedict's School

One day during a physical education lesson at St Benedict's School we had a running exercise followed by a short recovery break. I was exhausted after the run, so I lay down on the cold floor and I decided to close my eyes for a second and rest them. As soon as I had closed my eyes, I began to have some sort of weird dream. I saw a beautiful field of sunflowers, and there were clouds, sun and warm wind. I saw myself turn, hearing someone call me.

'What?' I asked. Then I felt scared, because I saw my dead aunt. But she looked so alive!

'Aunt, what is going on?' I asked, hugging her hard. I was sure it was a ghost. 'I cannot believe I saw your ghost,' I screamed aloud to myself. My aunt looked at me then said, 'Sweetie, I am not a ghost. YOU decided to join us.'

Just then, from nowhere, everyone else from my family who was dead came out to say hello to me. We all sat down together among the sunflowers and I started to cry. Then I felt someone shaking me hard. My friends eventually woke me up and I was really sweaty and was still lying on the floor of the school gym. Afterwards they explained what they had seen – they said that I had stopped breathing for a few seconds, but to me it seemed like ages.

I saw the light – Derby

One night I was driving home from university and I was in a near-fatal car accident. I had just picked up my four-year-old son from pre-school and we were chatting. My son was telling me about his day, and I must not have been paying attention to the road properly. We got to a crossroads near our house, and our car got hit by another car. We went flying into the air and rolled a few times, but as we were spinning I felt as though time was slowing down, and I began to see a strange light in front of me which then formed the shape of an angel as everything around me fell silent.

I woke up in a hospital three days later. Luckily the only injury I had was nerve damage and my son was completely unhurt as he was strapped into his car seat. I am sure that the angels protected me and my son that day.

WAS I WATCHED OVER? - MERRILL SCHOOL

In the summer of 2003 I turned 15. One day during that summer I was sitting and chatting with the group of people I hung around with on 'our' wall, which we kind of 'owned' while we were at Merrill School. All of a sudden I began to feel faint, things went dark and I started to topple. As I fainted, I fell off the wall onto the cobble. I proceeded to roll down the cobble, cracking the side of my head open. I was apparently out for about 10 to 20 minutes before I woke up and saw the whole school surrounding me, but before I was completely awake I saw the most beautiful angel standing above me – it must have been 9ft tall.

A few days later I went back to school, and I was shocked by the story my friends told me about what had happened that day. They said my lips had gone blue and I had stopped moving completely. It seems that I had nearly died, but for some reason I was able to wake up.

I believe that someone or something had watched over me and kept me alive. I do believe in angels and spirits watching over people, and maybe I had that experience – well, I certainly thought that I saw one as I awoke that day.

HEALING VISION - DERBY

When I was 13, I was a girl intent on suicide. My boyfriend had broken up with me and I couldn't cope with life.

One night, one of those spooky, seems-like-death-in-the-shadows kind of nights, I walked about three and a half miles towards the cemetery with a pocket-knife and a pocket full of black roses – I had decided to kill myself that night. I looked around in tears and lay down on an empty spot next to a statue of an angel with its hands clenched as though holding a baby.

I opened the pocket-knife, sobbing uncontrollably, and stared at it for about 10 minutes, during which time I reminisced about my life in fast flashes. Then I started cutting my wrists, starting from my vein line all the way up to my elbow. I did this to both of my arms. I was bleeding to death I don't remember what happened next, but the next thing I knew I was lying in the arms of the angel statue. I looked up, unsure whether I was alive or dead, and I saw water stains on its face as though it was crying. I looked at my arms. The cuts were still there but incredibly they were not bleeding. I felt them and they were smooth, as if I was looking at wounds that were not there.

I was sure I was not meant to die as something had somehow prevented me from succeeding, and I decided that instead I wanted to live, and I have never done anything so stupid since.

THE BEAUTIFUL WOMAN - DERBY

I had woken up as normal at 7 o'clock one morning and started getting dressed, then at 8 o'clock I set off down the road to my workplace, the Inland Revenue offices. I was fortunate because I was able to walk to work and I followed my usual route.

I had not been walking for very long when all of a sudden a car sped out from nowhere, hit me and threw me 10ft into the air. I have no memory of what happened over the next few seconds. I remember nothing from being hit to waking up on the pavement.

As I opened my eyes a beautiful woman came towards me, picked me up and walked with me across a magical field. The flowers had colours I had never seen before, and I felt so happy. The woman told me that it was not time for me yet but when it was, she would be there for me and would never leave my side. She then walked me towards a body lying on the ground and to my amazement I saw that it was mine! She told me to lie down beside myself and she would do the rest.

Suddenly I started coughing. I looked around me and saw that I was back in the road with paramedics surrounding me. They took me to the hospital, where they confirmed that I had been dead for seven minutes.

That first night, as I lay in my hospital bed, I looked up and I am sure that I saw the beautiful woman watching me and looking after me, just as she promised she would.

NOT HER TIME - DERBY

My mum told me this story several years ago, and it has always stuck with me. I'm not quite sure if this counts as an angelic appearance or not, but I think it does.

My mum has had incredibly bad feet problems for almost her entire life. They started when she was very young, so when she was in secondary school she went to the hospital for surgery on them. Everything was okay until they gave her the anaesthetic and she had a really bad allergic reaction to it. As the surgeons hurriedly tried to counteract what was happening, she died on the table for a minute from the severity of her reaction. She still remembers, to this day, that she rose up and could see her body from below, and as she was floating, calmly surveying the team of surgeons trying to revive her body, she saw her grandfather's spirit floating alongside her. He said to her, 'It is not your time. Your family still need you.'

As soon as he spoke those words my mum woke up back in her body, with a frantic group of medics around her. She believes, as do I, that it was an angel who saved her, and that it truly was the spirit of her grandfather.

HER LAST NIGHT ON EARTH? – DERBY

When my wife was about 19 years old she studied nursing in Derby. On one occasion she was suffering quite badly with her asthma and went home. She told her mum she did not feel very well and went to bed early.

In the middle of the night she awoke to the strangest sensation. She felt as if she had somehow left her body, and as she looked around in the gloom she saw herself lying in her bed with her arm dangling off it. Shocked and frightened, she came to the conclusion that she was dead, and decided that she should try and say her goodbyes while she still could. So she proceeded to go to her family members in the home to say her goodbyes as they slept. She remembers that she walked through locked doors as though they were not there.

She said a sad, loving goodbye to her parents and then she went to her sister's room, who had her child in a bed nearby. She floated down and kissed the child and she began to cry. She watched as the child woke up and told her mother she wanted a drink of water. Her sister took her to the kitchen, and at no point did either of them see my wife, or her spirit, who was standing right beside them in the room. Shocked that they could not see her, my wife took this as proof that she must have passed away, so she returned for one last look at her body.

As she stood looking at herself she began to pray that she would not be taken because she still had so much she wanted to do in life – she wanted to fulfil her father's dream of the family moving back to America. All of a sudden she felt a warm feeling completely envelop her and she felt herself back in her body.

That morning, over breakfast, my wife told her family what she had experienced the night before, but no one believed her. But when she spoke of what she had seen them do while she visited them, they began to believe that maybe something had happened to her, they just didn't know what. I believe my wife's incredible story, and I believe that she had a genuine near-death experience.

GUARDIAN – ASHBOURNE

On my way to work a few months ago I was driving towards Ashbourne from Markeaton island as I usually do. I am shamed to admit it, but I was tuning the radio at the time, which I know is a stupid and dangerous thing to do. I looked down to turn the dial, and when I looked up I found, to my terror, that I was on the wrong side of the road. Then, appearing in a flash and disappearing just as fast, I saw someone dressed all in white appear in the road.

I swerved back onto my side of the road and then I slowed to a stop. I frantically turned around and looked for somebody in the road, but there was no one around. I know what I saw and to this day I believe that what flashed up by my car was an angel protecting me and other drivers from harm and my stupidity.

TRUST AND YOU SHALL FIND – DERBY

I have a good friend called Anna and we have a mutual friend, Ellie. We have been close for many years and got to know each other's families very well too. When Ellie's mother died several years ago it hit us all very hard.

Anna decided to put some flowers on Ellie's mother's grave. She decided to go alone as she was close to Ellie's mother and wanted some time alone to pay her own resects. However, when she got to the graveyard she couldn't find the grave. She spent nearly an hour looking for it but still couldn't find it. While she was looking, she saw a man nearby visiting the grave of a loved one too. He looked at her and could tell by the look on her face that she was lost.

When Anna confirmed his suspicions he told her to think of the person she was trying to find, and their spirit would lead her to them. Anna said okay, but it must have sounded as if she did not believe it, so he told her that it really did work, before smiling and walking away.

Thinking that she had spent long enough looking in vain, Anna decided to try what the man had said. She thought about Ellie's mother as clearly as she could, and incredibly, just a few seconds later, she found the grave. Anna looked around the graveyard to thank the man, thinking that he could not have got far, but he was nowhere to be seen.

Anna did not believe in ghosts, spirits or anything paranormal before that day, but from then on she honestly believes that Ellie's mother's spirit guided her that day, after the kind man had given her some help.

A MIRACULOUS ENCOUNTER – DERBY

My great-great-great grandfather James was chopping firewood one day in 1822 when all of a sudden he accidentally struck his left shin with his axe, tearing the flesh and splintering the bone. With each beat of his heart, bright red blood gushed horribly from the wound, and all of his wife's efforts to stop the flow of blood were futile.

As he lay stricken on the floor, it appeared that he would not survive, when suddenly a handsome, grey-haired gentleman walked into the house uninvited and made his way straight into the room where James lay.

'How do you do, my good friend? You seem to be in trouble,' he said, his presence and cheery demeanour baffling both my great-great-great grandfather and his wife.

'Yes,' answered James, curtly, 'it looks as though my moments in this life are numbered.'

At this the old gentleman knelt down, took a small bottle from his pocket and handed it to James. 'Just apply this and the bleeding will stop,' he said, and then he just turned away and walked out of the room.

Puzzled, James called his wife and told her to follow the man and find out who he was. She hurried to the door but could not see him anywhere. Knowing that her husband was bleeding to death, she ran back in, grabbed the bottle that the man had given James and poured the contents onto his leg. Amazingly, James's leg stopped bleeding with the first application of the medicine, and his life was spared, but sadly he lost his leg.

He believed that the grey-haired gentleman was sent from heaven to save his life, and our family have ensured that every generation is told the story of how my great-great-great grandfather survived to help keep his memory alive, and that of the grey-haired man who saved him.

THE PARAMEDIC - DERBY

Six years ago my nephew, who is a paramedic, came to the city and stayed with me for the weekend. I was single at the time, and I had planned to go to a singles' dance on the Friday night. As he was single too, I asked if he would like to go, and he said he was excited to see what the dances were like in Derby. So we got ready and went out, and the dance was fun but nothing really exciting happened.

We got home to my flat at about 1am and sat down in my living room for a chat. After talking for half an hour there was a knock on the door. I got up to see who it was, and was surprised to see that it was my son, who was living with my ex-husband at the time. He told me that he had been in a play that evening and they had had a cast party close to my house, and rather than heading all the way to his dad's could he stay at mine. I said that was fine and he came in.

Now, I am a morning person, and I hate staying up late so I almost never do, but that night was different. The three of us stayed up talking about dreams, ghosts and other paranormal things, and we were all having a good time, chatting and laughing, until at about 3.45am I noticed my nephew was sat perfectly still as if he was frozen, not saying a word. Without warning, he jumped off the sofa, said he needed to go outside and walked out. I thought that it was strange as he had quit smoking several years before and I could not imagine why he would need to go outside.

About 15 minutes later he reappeared at the door with a young man who was wet and muddy from head to toe. He called me through from the living room and asked if the man could call his mother. I agreed, a little suspicious. My nephew told me that he had suddenly felt compelled to go outside, and he had no idea why. He went out, checked the locks on his car, looked up at the stars and then stood there until he heard a motorcycle go by, followed by the sound of it flipping over as it went around the corner. It was very dark, so my nephew grabbed a flashlight out of his car and went around the corner to look.

He shone the flashlight and saw a motorcycle on its side, and pinned underneath was a young man. My nephew grabbed the motorcycle off the young man and then explained that he was a paramedic and was there to help. Eventually he thought him stable enough to bring to the house.

The young man was in shock and he was badly injured. We called his mother and she came to fetch him and took him to the local hospital. Two days later she came over to see me. She told me that her son had broken his collarbone and several ribs, injured his leg, had several head injuries and internal bleeding. She said the doctor told her that if he had not been helped when he was, he would have certainly died.

The young man told his mother that he had been pinned under his motorcycle and was unable to free himself when my nephew had arrived and saved his life. She also told me that her son had been home only a week after returning from serving a mission for the church. She had asked him not to go out that night as she had had a bad feeling, but he went anyway, thinking she was being silly.

I now believe with all my heart that angels and guardians are watching over us, and that one told my nephew to run out of the house without warning that night.

HEALING POWER - ST MARY'S CHURCH, DERBY

I have a disability, so one day when I was very young my mother took me to a healing Mass with my grandmother at St Mary's Church in Derby.

While we were in the church I began to run around, and I fell, hit my head and split it open. My mother came over to check on me and took me to one side and sat me under a statue of Mary and Jesus while she went to get some help. Finding nobody about, she went into the bathroom to get paper towels to clean me up and then went to get my grandmother.

However, when they came back to where I was sitting they discovered I had no blood on my clothes or anything. My grandmother thought my mother must have been exaggerating, or that she was crazy, but my mother got the paper towels to prove to my grandmother that it had been bad and they were still bloody.

My mother asked me what happened, and I said, 'Jesus bleeds just like me, so he came down and took my blood away.' Which, I am sure you will agree, is a strange thing for a youngster to say.

HELP! - HARTINGTON STREET, DERBY

At the age of seven I recovered from pneumonia and had to be monitored throughout the night by my parents. In order to do this properly my parents moved my bed into their room so I was within easy reach.

One night while I was in there I woke up to see what I am sure was a Victorian girl standing at the bottom of my bed, trying to grab me. I began to feel very afraid as I realised it was not a dream, and I saw that she looked very sad and had long straggly hair, which draped over her face, and her eyes were very sullen. I grabbed my mum's hand which was hanging from the bed next to mine and the girl disappeared. As I was taking numerous pills at the time and was still very ill, everyone said it just was my imagination. I decided that they must be right, so I told myself that it was nothing and forgot about it.

Three years later, when I had fully recovered from my illness, I was sitting in the living room after school one day, watching TV. My mum said she was going to the shop and left me alone in the house.

Suddenly, from the corner of my eye, I saw the girl again. Terrified by the vision, I ran as fast I could out into the garden and waited for my mother to return. Yet again I was told it was my imagination and so again I forgot about it.

But less than one year later I encountered her again. I was lying in my bunk bed, and I suddenly woke up to find her on my ladder. She did not seem to want to hurt me and soon climbed down. As she did so I got a good look at her, and she was dressed in an old, black Victorian dress and still looked sad.

After my initial fear faded, I plucked up the courage to ask her who she was. She didn't tell me her name, but instead she told me how she died – she was murdered by her father when he came home drunk one night. Before I could say another word she disappeared right before my eyes.

I did some research and found out that the house was 120 years old and had been owned by a family called the Swinburnes. I often wonder if the little girl I saw in my childhood was a relative of theirs. Then my auntie told me that when she had slept in the house, she had seen the little girl and the floating head of a man with a big brown beard. I was shocked to hear this as Mr Swinburne had apparently been known for his huge beard. I knew then that the spirit needed help, and that must be the reason for her appearing to me. I decided that I had to do something about it, so I contacted a psychic who came in and told me that she had helped her towards the light. No one has seen her since that day.

THE SINGING MAN – LONG EATON

One day in 1989 my mother and I were driving through Long Eaton, when we saw a car crash just ahead of us. We pulled over to see if the driver and passengers were okay and we found that they were all fine except one man, who was badly injured.

I called an ambulance and as we waited I noticed that everyone was talking in a small group about the crash, but no one was tending to the wounded man, so I decided that I should see if he was alright. As I approached the car to talk with him and keep him calm, I saw that there was a tall man with slicked back hair wearing a business suit already with him. I was certain that he had not been with the wounded passenger a few seconds before, so I assumed he must have stopped his car to help but we had not noticed. I looked around for his car, but I saw only ours and the crashed ones.

I turned to look at him again, and I noticed that he was singing to the hurt man, and his voice was so beautiful. As I stepped closer I felt a warm aura around him and, strangely, I felt very calm and relaxed.

I stood behind him and said, 'Where did you – ?' But as I spoke to him he looked at me and I stopped talking. I became transfixed as I looked into his eyes; they were a very bright blue. There was something about them that stopped me from speaking.

He smiled at me and said, 'He will be fine. Don't worry.' He put his hand on my shoulder. 'Good boy. You did the right thing to care for him when others didn't.' He smiled at me, and I smiled back, then my mother called me over. I looked back at the blue-eyed man and he was gone. No one was there, and the warm feeling left me. I sighed and felt very sad. I never saw anything like that again, but somehow I knew that man was the injured man's angel.

FIRST DATE – SPONDON

When I was a teenager, during the 1970s, I lived in Spondon with my mum, dad and brother and we were an average family. My mother worked as a home help and my father worked on the railway, while I was at college studying to become a secretary.

One beautiful summer's evening I returned home from college and got ready for my first date with a new boyfriend, even though I had three hours before I was being picked up. I carefully did my hair and make-up, put on my best dress and boots and went downstairs to seek the approval of my parents. I still had two hours left to wait before Ian, my date, would be picking me up, and I must have paced the lounge carpet over and over again hoping that he would arrive early.

Ian was a lovely chap who worked hard as a ticket agent at Derby Station. I met him when I went to visit my dad at work one day and we immediately clicked. I was sure that it was love at first sight, but I would never have admitted it at the time for fear of being laughed at.

The other great thing about Ian was that he had a car! It sounds very boring now but in the 1970s cars were really expensive, so your dad would have a car but never your boyfriend. Ian loved his car, it was a maroon Allegro and he polished the bodywork so much that you could see your face in it. He was my first boyfriend with a car and I was keen for us to drive through the village so that some of my friends would notice us, giving me a chance to brag a bit for a change.

Right on time, Ian knocked on the door and I raced to greet him. After greeting my family, Ian and I stepped outside and into the car, ready to go, and I can still remember how excited I felt about it to this day. There was only one problem, though, I was too young to drink so that ruled out many places that you would usually go to on a date. After much discussion we decided to go to Matlock Bath, which has always been a favourite haunt of courting couples.

Driving through Spondon village in the car was fantastic, and just as I had predicted we turned many heads. We then drove past Locko Park and were both admiring the scenery when all of a sudden the sky turned black and the car cut out. We stopped for no apparent reason in the middle of the road. There seemed to be no life in the car at all and we both sat there rather gobsmacked by our situation. Poor Ian seemed paralysed from embarrassment.

Out of nowhere, a herd of deer ran across the road directly in front of the car. They seemed to be coming from all directions and were paying no attention to the road or our car. After about five minutes the herd had passed and the sky began to lift in colour, and then the car's engine began to start again all by itself. Completely bemused, we continued on our way.

We discussed what happened over and over again on that date, and the car never did cut out again. The only explanation that we could come up with was that his grandfather, who had passed away and had given Ian the car, was looking after us that night by making the car cut out, because if we had hit the deer we would definitely have been injured or maybe worse.

I am grateful to whoever or whatever was looking after us that night and Ian and I have now been married for over 30 years, but we might not have even got through the first date without that bit of divine intervention.

CHAPTER 6

PSYCHIC MESSAGES

So what exactly is a Psychic? According to the Oxford Dictionary it is: relating to or denoting faculties or phenomena that are apparently inexplicable by natural laws, especially involving telepathy or clairvoyance; a person appearing or considered to be telepathic or clairvoyant; of or relating to the soul or mind; a person considered or claiming to have psychic powers, a medium.

GYPSY ENCOUNTER - ALVASTON

My mother was not a superstitious woman and could have been described as a 'spade is a spade' type of lady who certainly didn't suffer fools gladly. We lived on Warren Street in Alvaston in a large but unimposing terrace house. One Monday my mother was scrubbing the doorstep, as she did every week, and it was not unusual for guests to be greeted by a view of my rather buxom mother's rear end as she knelt on all fours. As soon as she finished she came inside to make me a warm drink as I was off school with measles and was really quite poorly. Just as she was about to make the drink, however, there was a loud knock on the door and I can remember my mother cursing at the thought that someone was standing on her newly scrubbed step.

I followed her to open the door and hid behind her apron so that the visitor would not see that I was covered in spots. Standing on our doorstep was a very old woman, and I remember thinking she must be at least 100 years old. She immediately grabbed my mother's hand and began to speak before my mother could even react.

'I can see that you have two children,' the old woman said.

'Yes', my mother replied, a little taken aback and puzzled as to how she knew this or why she was saying it.

'Well one of them will be involved in a crash tonight, but they will be OK even though the doctors will think otherwise,' she said, to my mother's obvious horror. 'You must place your wooden cross in his hands and keep it there.'

Normally my mother would have sent such a woman away with a harsh word, but for some reason my mother continued to listen.

'Your daughter is unwell but will recover tomorrow and when she grows up she will be a nurse. You will also come into some money by the weekend,' the lady said in a soft voice.

The conversation continued for several minutes, and as she was turning to go my mother gave the old woman some change and in return the woman gave my mother a small bunch of clover.

My mother and I didn't speak about the old woman for the rest of the day, but at about 4pm there was a terrible banging on the door. When my mother opened it she saw one of my brother's friends standing on the doorstep, crying.

'William's been hit by a car,' he wailed as he and my mother ran up the street towards London Road, where a crowd had gathered around the mangled mess of my brother and his bike.

My brother had taken such a blow to the head that he was unconscious and the doctors were unsure if he would make it. My mother didn't believe a word of it and placed her little wooden cross in his hands, just as the gypsy woman had instructed her, and kept telling the doctors that he would be OK.

Thankfully for my mother, the next day I was feeling much better so she could focus all her attention on my brother. He regained consciousness after three days and had no after effects at all. Also, when I grew up I trained to be a nurse, so all of the old woman's predictions came true.

TESTING TIMES – DERBY

My mother was psychic and used to read for a number of ladies near to our home in the west end of Derby. It was not unusual for me to arrive home from school to find her surrounded by half a dozen women all wanting to know their fortune.

Her particular skill was psychometry and she could give a full reading just by holding on to an object that she had been given. I only saw it as a wonderful parlour game as she would always 'perform' it at Christmas or at family parties. She was so accurate that she sometimes could not believe the information she was able to pass on herself.

When I was in my 20s I happened to find an old tin button from a soldier's coat as I walked down St Peter's Street in Derby. I was curious about how it had got there and took it home with me. In order to find out its origins I decided to test out my mother's gift. I carefully wrapped the button inside a handkerchief so that it was an indistinguishable shape and not obviously a button. Thus camouflaged, I handed it to my mother.

To my surprise, as she held the handkerchief in her hands she started to cry. She described terrible war scenes and bloodshed and then threw the small package across the floor – I was amazed. I walked over and picked up the handkerchief containing the button then took it to a man in the old market hall who specialised in selling war memorabilia. He took one look and confirmed that it was indeed a military button from a World War Two army jacket – and I never again doubted my mother's ability.

A DATE WITH DESTINY – RIPLEY

I have two children, and my first was conceived with the help of fertility treatment after the consultants at the Derby City Hospital told me that it was very unlikely that I would ever be able to conceive naturally. Although the news was devastating I soon decided that as fertility treatment was my only option I had to go through with it. I soon gave birth to my first child.

Some years afterwards, in 2002, I was walking through Ripley town centre when an old woman approached me. She was only about 4ft tall and she smelt of lavender. She simply touched my arm, then whispered to me that I was pregnant.

I protested that I could not be but she simply smiled and walked away. I turned around to see where she went but I was amazed to find that she had vanished. There was no way that she could have turned off the road or gone into a shop in that short space of time.

Surprised by what the woman had said, curiosity eventually got the better of me and I went into a chemist and bought a pregnancy test, which to my amazement showed that I was indeed pregnant.

I gave birth to my second child, a daughter, and as she grew up it became apparent that she had the amazing gift of healing and psychic ability.

HOW DID SHE KNOW? – ALFRETON

Several years ago I went to see a clairvoyant called Libby with my work colleagues and I had been looking forward to it for weeks, hoping that she would be able to tell me that some good was going to come into my life after going through a very messy divorce.

My friends went in first and as I waited for my turn I became more and more excited because what she had told my friends seemed so accurate. Soon it was my turn and before I could take my coat off and make myself comfortable Libby turned to me and said, 'I can see you moving from the house you are in at present.'

'Impossible,' I replied, 'I will never move from my house as it was my parents' house and they passed it on to me, so I don't have a mortgage. You must be mistaken.'

'No, I can see you will be moving before the year is out,' she continued.

'Why would I want to move?' I asked tentatively, as Libby was a well-respected clairvoyant and her accuracy was well known.

'Shuffle the cards and we will try and find out,' she said as she handed me her cards.

As I shuffled them, one of the cards fell to the floor and Libby immediately picked it up. I noticed that it was a king.

'What falls to the floor, comes to the door,' she said. 'There is going to be a romance for you with a dark man and that is why you will move.' Slightly confused, I pressed her for more information, as getting involved in a romance was the last thing on my mind after only just setting myself free from a miserable marriage.

'That is all I can see on that subject,' she said as she went on to tell me other things, which to this day I cannot remember.

I gave her the agreed fee and got up to rejoin my friends, who were waiting outside. As I did so she said, 'The new house will be further away from the road than the one you are in.' And on that note I left the room.

When I got home my children laughed at me for wasting money on going to see a fortune teller. I was not totally sure whether I had wasted my money either because to be honest I didn't think I would ever move from my house in Alfreton.

I forgot the reading until six months later. It was winter, and as I sat watching television one night there was a loud knock at the door. Getting up to investigate, I saw a large man standing on the doorstep.

'I'm sorry for disturbing you, but I want to buy a property in this area and your house caught my eye.' He said in a well spoken voice.

'The house isn't for sale,' I replied.

'Oh that is a shame because it is exactly what I am looking for – would you mind if I came in for a moment.'

Now normally I would not have let a strange man into the house, but for some reason I found myself inviting him in – I guess with two teenagers in the house I did not feel alone. The man explained that he was a property developer and had been looking in the area for a house to renovate and then rent out, and as my house was a three-storey building it would be perfect.

'Would you mind showing me around the house?' He asked.

'Not at all,' I replied, 'just remember I have no intention of selling.' I showed him around the house then we went to the kitchen where I made him a cup of tea.

'If ever you do decided to sell, I would offer you £250,000 for the house and would pay your moving fees. I would turn this into a number of flats,' he continued.

Again I told him I would not be selling but he gave me his number just in case.

After he left I spoke to the kids about what he had said and they suggested that it wouldn't do any harm to get a local estate agent to come round and value the house. So the next day I phoned and arranged the valuation, only to find out that the house was worth just £160,000. I talked to my kids and they thought that I would be mad not to sell as it would give us enough money to buy another house and pay off all my debts, so I called the man back and told him I would sell to him for £250,000.

The man was true to his word and I took on the task of trying to find a suitable house for my family. Within a week I found our dream house, which was set away from the road just as Libby had predicted, and the sale of the houses went through without a hitch.

We moved into our new house and I felt liberated when I paid off all my debts, determined that it would be a fresh start for the whole family. I started to feel that my life was back on track even if there was still no sign of the romance that Libby had promised.

After we had lived in our new house for about a year, I was woken up in the night by an almighty crash. I ran to the bedroom window and saw that a car had driven through our fence at the end of the garden. I immediately got dressed and ran outside to see if anyone had been hurt, which thankfully they had not.

Inside the car were two men in their 40s and they explained that they had been on their way to work when they had skidded off the road.

Clearly shaken, I invited them into the house and gave them a cup of tea. They wrote down their contact details so I could arrange for the fence to be repaired and left. A week later, with the new fence in place, I received the biggest bunch of flowers, which had been sent by the driver of the car, so I found his number to call him to thank him.

When I called him, he seemed really pleased to speak to me and asked if he could take me out for a meal to thank me for being so understanding, and as I had not been out for ages I agreed.

We got on like a house on fire and our friendship soon blossomed to romance and we have been together ever since. Everything that Libby told me came true, despite it seeming so far-fetched at the time of my reading, and now I really believe that good things come to those who wait.

CHAPTER 7

This chapter is dedicated to the loved ones who have passed over and those who are still alive.

MESSAGE IN THE MIRROR - CHESTER GREEN

I live in Chester Green, which is a well-known area in Derby for sightings of ghostly Roman soldiers, although I have never seen one.

My house is a traditional terrace and I live alone with my two cats and one dog, which have become my main companions since my mother passed away in the early summer. I missed my mum terribly at first and would often find myself crying over the slightest reminder of her, whether it be a song on the radio, a flower or even just the mention of her name. I struggled to get over my grief and wondered if my life would ever get back to some sort of normality.

My mother left me her engagement ring, which was a beautiful diamond and ruby ring that I wore with pride every time I went out so that I could feel close to her. I wore it to the Assembly Rooms when I went to see a concert and came home to discover that I was no longer wearing it, and I was even more distraught. I phoned the Assembly Rooms but they said they had not found it, and I contacted the bus company I had been travelling with but again I got the same response. So I had to deal with the fact that I would never see the ring again and this only added to my grief.

Several months passed and I was feeling particularly low as my mother's birthday was approaching and it would be the first one without her. I decided to run a bath hoping that a bit of relaxation would help me. As I ran it, the bathroom window and mirror clouded over with the steam from the bath. I lowered myself into the water and cried my eyes out.

As I lay in the tub, out of the corner of my eye I noticed something on the mirror. It seemed that the condensation had not covered the entire mirror and it looked odd, so I climbed out of the bath to investigate. As I got closer I saw that written in the condensation were the words 'Ring in pipe.' I stood there dripping wet wondering what it could mean, not even stopping to think how on earth the writing appeared on the mirror in the first place.

As I stood there, I remembered the lost engagement ring, so I grabbed a towel and ran straight down to the kitchen sink. I opened the cupboard beneath it and started taking off the pipes one by one, which is something I had never done before. There, incredibly, at the bottom of the pipe was my mother's engagement ring!

This time I was crying tears of joy as I really believed my mother had written the message on the mirror as she knew what the ring meant to me. Though, if that is not strange enough, I still cannot explain how it got there inside the pipe as I always wear rubber gloves when I wash the dishes and the holes in the plughole are too small for a ring to pass through them. I can only think that my mother put the ring there for me to find and I am very grateful that she did.

A SPECIAL BOND - ALLESTREE

When my father's condition deteriorated as he had cancer, we could do no more than make him comfortable and wait for the inevitable to happen. The night before his death I was with him in the hospital and saw his soul moving away from his body. I kissed his head, wished him well on his journey and left knowing that tomorrow would be the end of his life and the beginning of our lives without this wonderful man.

The next morning I dressed and left the house early to be with my father. I was prepared mentally that this would be his last day and I wanted to spend as much time as possible with him, but it was not meant to be. When I arrived at the hospital the duty nurse informed me that my father had passed away moments before I arrived. It was a strange experience because although I was obviously very sad at my father's passing I also felt a sense of relief that he was not suffering anymore, and to be honest the feeling of relief also came with the feeling of guilt for feeling this way. It was a strange mix, which I am sure many people have experienced when they have lost a loved one who has suffered for so long.

I went in to see my father and he seemed totally at peace, the pain that had ravished him for many years seemed to have been erased from his face and he looked many years younger than he had done when he was alive. I kissed him and the doctor signed the death certificate and I drove home in silence.

On arriving at my home in Allestree I realised that I would have the task of telling my son, who was only 10, that his grandfather had died, and I contemplated how would be the best way to tell him as he had never experienced death before.

It was still very early when I turned the key in the door and the rest of the house were just getting up and ready for the day ahead. As I came into the lounge my son saw me.

'Mum, I had the strangest dream last night. I dreamt that grandad visited me and he sat me on his knee and told me that it was time for him to go and that he wanted me to be a good boy and tell you that he is no longer in pain. He also said that he had seen his friend Ida and I was to tell you this. Then he disappeared, Mum, and I saw myself crying,' my son said to me with a calm voice far beyond his years.

I scooped him in my arms and told him that his grandad had indeed died and thanked him for telling me that he was not in pain and that he was with Ida.

Then it suddenly dawned on me...how on earth did my son know about Ida? She had been my father's neighbour and had died when I was a little girl, and as far as I can remember we had never spoken about her. It left me with no doubt that my father had visited my son to say goodbye.

The following week we were arranging the funeral when my son came downstairs from his room and told me that he had seen his grandad again playing with his toys. One of the greatest regrets that my father had was that he was too ill to play with the toys with his grandson and it gave me comfort to know that he was doing this now.

'Grandad also said that he knows you have ordered red roses for the top of his coffin, but he would really like orange lilies as these were his favourite.'

I had no doubt that my son was telling me the truth because he had been upstairs when I called the florist and arranged a floral tribute of red roses and I had completely forgotten that my father's favourite flowers were orange lilies. I immediately phoned the florist back to change the order to my father's wishes.

My father appeared to my son on many occasions throughout his childhood, and many years later, when my son married, he told me that he was sure he had seen his grandad sitting at the back of the church, smiling.

UNCLE PETER – BELPER

When I was about five my Uncle Peter died. When we went to visit his grave recently in Belper, I was shocked to see what looked like a black shadowy figure standing behind his gravestone.

Shaken by the eerie sight, I walked over to investigate, but when I got close to the grave the black figure disappeared into thin air. I was so scared that I nearly wet myself! I ran as fast as I could to tell my mum what I had seen but she didn't believe me.

Now, every time we drive by the graveyard where my uncle is buried I always see the black shadowy figure hovering right above his grave, but I am the only one who sees it.

UNCLE GHOST - DERBY

My Uncle Jerry died in the early 1990s. He was a man loved by everyone and he was very kind.

One night a little while after he had died I had an argument with my parents and stormed out of the house in a fit of rage. Nobody seemed to understand me like my Uncle Jerry and he had left me feeling very alone. I ran to his grave in Milford, sat there and moaned almost all evening, not caring that my parents would probably be worried sick and out looking for me.

Through the sound of my angry tears, I heard a voice say, 'It's okay, child, brighter skies will come,' which was what my uncle told me every time I was sad. I looked around and couldn't believe my eyes. There, standing by the side of the grave, was a ghostlike figure on the cold icy ground that looked just like my Uncle Jerry. Then he disappeared.

I had the urge to return home straight after that, and as soon as I got in the door I blurted out that I had seen my Uncle Jerry to my parents. They were really confused but didn't say anything as I think that they were just glad that I was feeling better and home safely.

Now, every time I am feeling down I visit his grave, but unfortunately he has never come through to help me again.

GRANNY - DERBYSHIRE

My great-great-grandmother lived in a small village in Derbyshire all her life. One cold, stormy November night many years ago my great-great-grandmother was on her deathbed, with all of the family gathered at the house to say their final farewells to her.

Granny, as she was known by everyone, was lying in the same bed where she had given birth to her five children. Now, instead of a new life being brought into the world, hers was being taken. She had been sick for quite some time and we knew that she would not be around much longer.

During the night the wind was shaking our old farmhouse. There were noises outside, and the limbs of the trees were popping and snapping. Suddenly, out of the darkness, there was a knock at the door. My great-great-grandpa was surprised but thought that it was maybe a family member coming to see Granny so he got up and answered it. However, when he got to the front door he found no one there; there was nothing but darkness. He closed the door and thought that maybe it was just a tree branch hitting the house. After about 30 minutes there was another knock at the door. Grandpa opened it and once again to his surprise no one was there.

He thought about it for a minute and knew that nobody could run fast enough to get off the porch and out of sight before he answered the door, so he kept a look out of the front window, waiting and watching for someone to knock and run.

Another 30 minutes past, and once again there was a knock at the door, this time louder then the others. Grandpa, angry and a little scared, opened the door and yelled, 'In the name of God, take what you want and leave!'

At that very moment my great-great-grandmother drew her last breath and departed this world. She died with a peaceful smile on her face.

You may call it coincidence, but my family has always believed that the mysterious knocks were an angel coming to take Granny into the next life.

EERIE PHONES – DERBY

One day in about 2000 I was sitting at my computer, talking to a friend about how I was coping with the recent death of my nephew, and all of a sudden I heard the sound of a phone ringing. At first I thought nothing of it, until I remembered that the phone had stopped working several days before and had been disconnected. My next thought, as it continued to ring, was that maybe someone had plugged it back in and reconnected it to the phone line, so I left my computer to check it, but it was still disconnected.

A few days later I was sitting at my computer again, and again the broken, disconnected phone started to ring. This time I picked it up and tried to answer it, but of course it would not switch on. I told my sister, my nephew's mother, about what had happened with the phone and her reply really gave me the creeps. She told me that she had had the same thing happen to her on a phone that she had thought broken. She said to answer it if it rang again as if it was a normal call. A few days later the phone did ring again, while I was sitting at my computer. This time I answered it, but I got no answer to my tentative hello.

All I could think was that it was my nephew trying to contact us since it also happened to my sister.

HOPE FROM A FRIEND – DERBY

A few years ago one of my close friends passed away. When I found out that I was pregnant soon afterwards, I could not help but think about my friend – I started to think about her every day.

Nine months later I gave birth to my daughter, but to my horror the doctors told me that she was not breathing. I started to cry with panic at the news, and as the doctors frantically tried to revive my little girl I looked up and was amazed to see my friend standing over my daughter, staring at her with tears in her eyes. Then I heard the most beautiful sound I have ever heard – the sound of my daughter crying.

I believe to this day that if it was not for my friend's spirit, my daughter would not be here today. I thank my friend every night before I go to bed as I believe it was her who gave my daughter her life.

BROTHERLY ANGEL – ALFRETON

My story begins in Derbyshire, Alfreton to be precise, which had been my family's home for as long as I could remember. I lived there with my brother, mum and dad, until I married and moved to California in 2005.

While I lived at home my youngest brother, who had always been very spiritual and wise beyond his years, suddenly developed cancer. Despite this, our hopes remained high that he would recover.

I wanted to give him something that reflected his faith, so I went to a little crystal shop in Cromford, where I found an angel statue which I gave to him for comfort. He adored the angel and kept it by his bedside, and he even took it with him whenever he went into hospital for treatment.

A short while later he found a photograph in a book of an angel statue in Italy that, incredibly, looked just like him. It had his face and features, and the statue I had given him turned out to be a reproduction of exactly the same angel. Sadly my brother died from his cancer a few months later,

141

and my parents wanted me to have the angel back as a reminder of my brother. Not long afterwards I met and married my husband, and because of his work we had to move to California. I hated the thought of leaving my parents, but with the internet we could communicate daily and they promised they would come over and visit me. I took the angel statue with me and placed it in my front yard as soon as I arrived.

Now, I don't know if you will recall, this but there was a terrible fire in Pioneertown, California, in 2006, and many homes were destroyed. The entire neighbourhood, which was where I was living, had to be evacuated, and we took refuge in temporary shelters for several days.

When I was allowed to go back to my old farmhouse, expecting the worst, I found that my home was miraculously untouched by the fire. The flames had stopped right at the feet of the angel statue. Ours was the only house in the area that was 100 per cent undamaged.

The firemen could not explain why the fire did not take my home. The flames just didn't move beyond the statue. They told me it was a miracle it did not burn to the ground, let alone escape completely undamaged. The statue, incredibly, is not even scorched.

HOSPITAL ANGEL – DERBY ROYAL INFIRMARY

My family and I are very religious and coming from the Caribbean community in Derby we spent a great deal of time in church when we were not visiting my father in hospital. When my father first fell ill with congenital heart failure, he was admitted to Derby Royal Infirmary.

One night, way past visiting hours, he was reading his Bible as he was scared about of his condition. He got as comfortable as he could get, not being in his own bed, and eventually fell asleep, but he awoke in the middle of the night to see a human figure standing at the foot of his hospital bed. He later said the figure was dressed in white and had a strange glow. He was half awake so he thought he was just seeing one of his nurses checking up on him, and he fell back to sleep with a calmness he had not felt since his diagnosis.

The next morning, he asked all of the nurses who had been in his room in the middle of the night, but they had all been doing other things at the time he saw this being at the foot of his bed. The nurses told him that they had no reason for coming into his room through the night because they were watching his vital signs at the nurses' station, and apparently they had been fine the entire night.

My dad believed till the day he passed away that he had been visited by an angel. He had never felt so much peace than he did when he saw the being at the foot of his bed. The angel said nothing to him, but it was there, just watching over him. It must have been his guardian angel.

'NO, NOT NOW...WAIT! - DERBY

My stepfather Bill had cancer, and after a losing a year-long battle with the condition he finally ended up in a hospice as he succumbed to the disease. He had had a tough marriage and a hard life before I knew him and I could not help but think that he had been through so much in his life that it was unfair he was faced with the painful death that cancer brings.

When I visited him at the hospice, most of our conversations were about the existence of an afterlife; he was so terrified of dying and for some reason he thought that I might have some answers for him. While all this talk seemed to comfort him somewhat, he could never let go of his fear. He lived several more weeks at the hospice, which was unexpected, most likely because he clung to life so hard, afraid of what would happen in death.

I was not present, but the night he died a priest was there to read him last rites, along with the nursing staff and several members of my family. They began to pray around his bedside when his condition worsened, and during the prayer, Bill abruptly opened his eyes, lifted his hand up to the ceiling and smiled, then he died. It was as if in the end he had been given a chance to see there was nothing to be scared about and finally was able to let go of life.

At the funeral, I passed this information on to one of his daughters from his previous marriage, to give her some comfort from it as well. To my great surprise, she looked startled and ran from the church.

Stunned at her reaction, I followed her outside and asked her why she was so upset by what I had said. She told me tearfully that she had been in Bill's hospice room a week earlier, and in the middle of their conversation he looked up to the ceiling. She told me that he had lifted his hand up and clearly heard him say, 'No, not now...wait!' Then, when he looked back down at her, she asked him what he was doing, and he said he did not remember doing it.

I am a firm believer now in an afterlife and that there is no pain during death. It was Bill's last gift to me, and, hopefully, now to you.

A VOICE IN THE NIGHT - WIRKSWORTH

Years ago a couple of friends and I used to do some amateur ghost-hunting. We used to sit in our car with tape recorders in a clearing in the woods by my house in Wirksworth at night.

One night we were waiting there as usual when a car pulled up about 50ft from us, and it stayed there for about half an hour. Then, just as suddenly as it had arrived, it drove away. We didn't think too much of it until the following night, when exactly the same thing happened again. This went on every day for a week.

Finally, on the last ghost-hunt of that week, I bravely went up to the car and knocked on the door. I was more than a little nervous as the window wound down. What would I be faced with? To my relief, I saw a perfectly normal looking man in the driver's seat. I asked him what he had been doing here each night, and he said that this was the place where his wife and children had been in a bad car accident and had died instantly. He said that each night he came to the spot to hear a little voice calling out, asking for his daddy. He heard it very clearly, but only in that spot.

Since that night we never saw the man again, and I hope that he found peace after all he went through.

GRANDAD WATCHING OVER US - ALLESTREE

I had just got a new digital camera for my college course and I was on my way home, back to Allestree, taking pictures on my journey. I didn't expect them to be any good when I put them on my PC the following day, but how wrong I was.

I had taken a picture of my mate Josh, and when I looked at the photograph on the computer I saw, sitting next to him on the bench, was a ghost! I immediately called Josh, who raced round to my house to have a look. I was amazed when he burst into tears after looking at it and said that the ghost looked like his grandad, who had died the year before.

Clearly upset by the photograph, I walked him back home and we showed it to his mum. She looked stunned and immediately went to a drawer and pulled out a photograph of her dad, and I could not believe it when I saw that he looked the same as the ghost in the picture I took.

GRANDAD'S SURPRISE VISIT – CROMFORD

One night I was staying at my boyfriend's house near Cromford, and as we were not allowed to share the same room he had given up his bed and was sleeping on the sofa downstairs.

I was trying to get to sleep, but because it was not my own bed I tossed and turned all night trying to get comfortable. I was turning over for what seemed like the hundredth time, when out of the corner of my eye I saw something that made me freeze with shock. I turned to get a closer look, hoping that the figure next to me was just my boyfriend, but to my amazement I found myself looking at a man with a longish beard and long hair. He wore jeans, braces and a white shirt and had glasses hanging out of his shirt pocket. Amazingly, although I felt shock at his sudden appearance, I didn't feel scared, I just smiled at him and he smiled back at me.

The next morning I told my boyfriend what I had seen. He looked stunned when I finished my description, and without saying a word he got out a photograph of exactly the same man. It was his grandfather. It seems that his dead grandfather had been giving me the once over, seeing if I was good enough for his grandson!

THE BACK SEAT

A few years ago my mother and I were coming back from my nan's funeral in Newcastle to Derby, and we were using my nan's old car. We had just turned off the motorway, when I heard a noise coming from the back. I thought nothing of it and went back to reading my magazine, but when I heard it another couple of times I started to get a little freaked out.

Confused, I turned to look into the back of the car – which was of course meant to be empty – but to my amazement, my nan was sitting in the back seat staring at me.

I screamed and told my shocked mum. She had to pull over as I was that scared I was physically sick. When we dared to look a second time, she was gone, but I had nightmares for about three weeks after that.

KNOCKS OF SORROW - FRIARGATE

I used to have a boyfriend from Iraq, and our souls were really closely connected, so when something happened to one of us the other would somehow know. After a while my boyfriend had to return to his home country for family reasons. I was sad to see him go, but he promised that he would be back to see me soon.

One night I was lying in bed and heard something knocking on the balcony window of my flat in Friargate. I wondered if somebody was there, but then I realised that the only entrance to the balcony was through my room.

I decided to leave it as it was probably nothing, but eventually, when it didn't stop, I knew that I had to investigate. I opened the door to look out and saw that nobody was there. I went back to bed, but the knocking started again, and I was really scared because I had a feeling that something was very wrong. I was so concerned that I called my parents, even though it was the middle of the night, because I just needed to speak to someone. They told me to try and get some sleep and that it would probably be OK in the morning. They were so wrong.

The next day my boyfriend's parents sent me a terrible message via email to tell me the love of my life had died, and I don't know if he had been trying to communicate with me that night, one last time.

THUMP, THUMP, THUMP - ALVASTON

A little while ago my parents and I moved into my grandad's house in Alvaston as he was getting frail and needed us to help look after him. One night I was sleeping peacefully in the room that I had been given in the house, when suddenly I heard three thumping noises coming from somewhere in the room, and then I heard what sounded like a high-pitched click.

I paid no attention to it and tried to sleep, but I found I couldn't because of a cold shiver down my face and ear. I looked up to see what had caused it and saw my grandad floating over my head! I flew out of my bed, ran downstairs and spent the rest of the night on the sofa. Later that night, when I had calmed down enough to sleep, I had a dream that my grandad had died.

When I woke up the next morning, my parents told me that my grandad had died in the night, and I worked out it must have been at about the same time that I saw him floating above my bed.

Hello, Daddy! – Derby

My father was a serviceman and a couple of years ago he was killed while serving in Iraq. After the news came through I was inconsolable and fell into a deep depression. It got so bad that I wouldn't eat or talk, and my condition was made worse when my mum decided that we needed to move to Derby so that she could be near her relatives. I felt like we were leaving my father's memory behind.

We had not been in the new house long when early one morning I felt something nudge me on my shoulder. I thought it was my mum waking me up for school, so ignored it. When it happened again I rolled over to snap at my mother's persistence, but when I did so I was faced with what looked like the figure of a man sitting next to me on the bed. I screamed with fright and covered my face with the blanket.

As I lay quivering beneath the covers, I heard a voice say, 'My baby girl, don't worry about me. I'm in a better place. Tell your mum I'm sorry for what I put her through, and that I will always love her. I will always be watching. I love you, baby girl.' Then all was quiet. I quickly uncovered my head to try and get another glimpse of the figure, which I was now sure was my father, but he was gone. I will always remember him coming to comfort me and telling me he was OK and not to worry.

New Year's call – Derby

My Uncle David died in October 2007 when he and his friend were drunk and had been driving on the wrong side of the road. They hit another car head-on, and my uncle died from the impact while his friend died from loss of blood.

A few days after the funeral my grandfather and I were sitting watching TV and talking about some of the good times we had shared with my uncle. We had been talking for most of the evening, when all of a sudden his mobile phone started to ring. As my grandfather was obviously tired, I offered to answer it for him, I walked over and picked up the phone, and, to my great surprise, the number and name on the screen said 'David.' Puzzled, I asked my grandfather whether Uncle David's phone was still in use. He said not and asked me to pass over the phone, which I did. He picked it up, and answered it by saying, 'David, is it you? Son, talk to me. I miss you so much!'

When he hung up the phone, I asked if there was any reply but my grandpa had only heard heavy breathing. We both cried, and it was quiet for a long time after that.

For some reason we both believe that my uncle did call that night, and we believe he did so because he had died without a goodbye to anybody in the family.

A little while later we wanted to know for sure whether he did or didn't call so we contacted the phone company, and they said someone had called from that number, but the number was not in service. I have no idea how to explain what happened.

OUR GRANDAD – DERBY

My cousin Chelsea and I were only nine when our grandad passed away. He was the life and soul of the family, and he was always very loving and knew how to have fun.

Before he died he had been very ill for a long time, and one day I watched as my aunt took his temperature – it was 99.7 degrees. We took him straight to the DRI because the doctor had said that if he came down with the slightest fever then they needed to know about it. Sadly, he never left the hospital. He began to deteriorate and about a month later he passed away, and it was then that strange things started to happen.

One day, a little while after my grandad had passed away, my aunt was not feeling well. She took out the thermometer and took her temperature. When she took the thermometer from under her tongue she realised that she too had a temperature of 99.7. Just as she was contemplating the coincidence, she saw the ghost of my grandad standing at the bottom of her bed. After her initial shock faded, the ghost indicated to her to sit outside.

She could hardly move, but felt that she had to obey, so she walked downstairs and sat on the kitchen step. Now, next to the kitchen step there was a rose bush that my grandad had given her for her birthday and it was still in bud. My aunt leant over to have a look at a bud, and all of a sudden it opened into full bloom before her very eyes. She immediately told her husband and he cut the rose and placed it on her bedside table.

Within a few hours her temperature had returned to normal and she swore it was down to her dad and the rose. To this very day we keep the rose in a little box. The petals are dried, but the rose is still bright red.

MY BEAUTIFUL MOTHER - DERBY

When I was about two or three years old, my mother died in a horrible car accident. My sister, my brother and I continued living with my dad in Derby for the next year and a half. Unfortunately, my dad was an alcoholic and had no idea how to take care of us alone and after a few bad incidents, the three of us were put into a foster home.

My brother, who was 15 at the time, returned to be with my dad and my sister, who was about 13, didn't want to leave me so we stayed together in the foster home. We were later adopted by neighbours, who lived just a couple houses down from my dad and brother, but still I very rarely saw my dad.

The years passed and I couldn't remember my mother's face apart from seeing it in photographs. I didn't like to ask about her as I felt that my foster mother was uncomfortable talking about her.

One day I had been looking at one of my few pictures of my birth mother, and I decided to go outside and sit in the front garden as it was a nice day and I wanted to go and think about her. As I sat down on the grass, out of the light stepped a beautiful woman, and as soon as I saw her I knew exactly who she was – it was my birth mother. She had her arms wide open as if she wanted me to come to her, so I walked slowly towards her and hugged her for ges. She didn't say anything to me; she just held me with a tearful smile on her face. She was wearing a long, white gown that touched the ground and swayed as she walked. On her head she was wearing a pretty white hat, and from the hat you could see her curly black hair which flowed a little below her shoulders.

I have told only a few people about the dream – my sister and a few friends. My sister tells me that she loved me with all her heart. I am the only one out of the three of us who has had such an experience.

R.I.P. - DERBY

My Aunt Norma Jean passed away on 15 April 2005 in Derby. She was 31 and too young to go.

My mother, little sister and I moved into her house about three weeks after she passed. It was a lovely house, and was full of little quirks; for example, there were window-shaped holes in the walls that connected the entrance and the living room.

We had only been living in the house a few weeks, when I was sitting on the sofa facing the odd wall and was on the phone to my boyfriend while I half-heartedly did my homework. My eyes were hurting as I was working on a laptop, so I looked up at the wall to give them a rest from the screen and screwed my eyes up a few times. For a brief moment I could have sworn that I saw my aunt in the entranceway window hole. I was very shaken and started to cry from shock, but my boyfriend eventually calmed me down and I told him what had happened.

After that night I did not see her again, but instead I felt her around me and odd things often happened. A couple of nights after my 18th birthday I was sleeping on the sofa, with my back facing outward. I started to drift off, and I was woken by the feeling of someone or something sitting right next to my legs at the foot of the couch. My initial thought was that it was just my sister's cat, so I told her to go away and to go sleep on my sister's bed, but I felt nothing when I tried to kick her off. When I looked up, I saw that the doors to the lounge were closed, so there was no way anyone could have got in. Just then I heard my aunt whisper my name in my ear and there was no mistaking it was her!

I now refuse to sleep on my own and always have all the lights on in the house before I go to bed!

THE VOICE ON THE PHONE – DERBY

My grandfather passed away during 2001. One day, not long after he died, I needed to phone my uncle, who was and still is living in my grandparents' house. The phone rang and a male voice answered. It said hello in a voice that sounded like my grandfather's. He had a very distinctive voice and I knew that it was certainly not my uncle.

Thinking I was just imagining things, I called the number back and the same thing happened again, and once again I hung up. Wanting to prove to myself that I was just imagining it all, I had my two eldest daughters call the number. I didn't tell them why I wanted them to call, and once they had done so I asked them what they heard. They both told me exactly what I expected: they heard a male voice saying hello, and then the answer machine kicking on about 30 seconds later.

A few days later I told my uncle about what happened, and I was amazed when he told me he was not even home that day. All we could think was that my grandfather was still answering his phone like he had done when he was alive, even though he had passed away.

Garage door goodbye - Derby

When my grandmother died it took a long time for my mum, aunt and other family members and I to go through her house to finally clean everything and get the house sold. After months of sorting through her belongings we finally had an offer from a buyer, and the sale went through without a hitch soon afterwards. My mum, sister and I were doing a final walkthrough to make sure that nothing was left and everything was perfect for the new owners. We had modernised the kitchen and bathroom, and in fact everything else in the house, including the garage door.

We were halfway out of the driveway, saying a tearful goodbye to our grandmother's old house, when the garage door suddenly shot back up after my mum had closed it on the way out. My mum parked the car, walked up to the door and pulled it back down. She got back into the car and again, as we were almost out of the driveway, it shot back up again. Then incredibly it began to go berserk. It was opening and closing all by itself and would then freeze halfway open before slamming shut again.

It finally stopped when we all said at the same time that we loved my grandmother and goodbye.

A beautiful reminder - Duffield

One spring morning when I was about 12 I awoke to be told that cleaning was my agenda for the day: my mum, brothers, sister and I were all cleaning the house from top to bottom. We went through every room, and finally we came to my parents' room to take the rugs out. Their bedroom window was shut because the lock had rusted and it refused to open, which was not unusual as they were the original sash windows and we couldn't have them replaced.

When we managed to free the rugs from under the furniture, we left the bedroom, closing the door behind us. When we later retuned to put things back to where they had been, however, there was a sweet smelling aroma of lilacs and fresh flowers which enveloped the whole bedroom.

At first we assumed that it was a perfume spray, but we couldn't find the bottle or spray can. We stayed in there for about two minutes, puzzled as to how the smell got there. We left the room to return to our spring cleaning, and mum was the last one out, closing the door behind her. Then, about five to 10 minutes later, she called us back to her room and told us that the smell had gone. There was no lingering scent of the lilacs we first smelled, considering we had left the room only minutes earlier.

Later that day mum remembered it was the anniversary of her grandmother's death, and she went on to explain to us how she had always loved the smell of lilacs and fresh flowers. I guess it was a beautiful reminder from a beautiful person that she is keeping a watchful eye over us.

CHAPTER 8

DOPPELGANGERS

A doppelganger, also spelt doppelgaenger, is said to be the ghost of a living person or any other sort of physical double. The idea of a doppelganger is similar to that of an 'evil twin'. The word doppelganger comes from the German *doppelgaenger*, literally meaning 'double-goer.'

There are many different types of doppelganger, and the definition of the term has become a grey area, with the meaning now generally encompassing any sort of double. The doppelganger may be ghostly or appear in the flesh. It may also be an 'evil twin' unknown to the original person who causes mischief by confusing friends and relatives, or it may be the result of the original person being in two places at once through an act of sorcery.

Throughout history there have been many stories about doppelgangers, especially concerning the practice of witchcraft and in folklore, and the doppelganger is said to have no shadow or reflection, much like vampires in some traditions. Doppelgangers are often malicious or a bad omen, and they can haunt their earthly counterparts. They may also give bad advice or put thoughts into their victims' heads which are not in their best interests.

Seeing your own doppelganger or the doppelganger of a friend or relative is considered very bad luck, and in some cultures they believe that it often heralds death or serious illness of the doppelganger's original. Cheery little thing then, wouldn't you say?

TAKE TWO - DERBY

One morning a few years ago, while my daughter was watching her favourite show on TV, she happened to look up and glance at her nanny, who was busy browsing some magazines in the same room. My daughter then stood up from the bed to heed the call of nature. Since the bathroom upstairs was being repaired, she had to use the other bathroom which was downstairs.

While she was going down the stairs, she was quite surprised to see her nanny already there, apparently washing the dishes. She did a double take and called her nanny in the bedroom twice. Her nanny then responded, and indeed she was still upstairs! This sent chills down her spine, and she ran back upstairs to tell the rest of the family the story.

TRACEY - DERBY

About 10 years ago, when I was 17, I was living in a hostel for young people close to the city of Derby. I was sitting in the communal room one Sunday in a seat next to a staff member, who was watching snooker on the television.

On Sundays usually no one was in at the hostel, so I was the only resident that day. From the corner of my eye I saw another resident, Tracey, enter the kitchen, get herself a drink of water from the taps, wash the glass, set it down and leave. I found this puzzling as I was sure she was meant to be at her mother's, so I asked the staff member beside me how long Tracey had been in. To my surprise he stated that she had been out all day. I explained that I had seen her right there in the kitchen, and he assured me that he heard someone in the kitchen too but it could not have been Tracey.

I know what you are thinking, it must have been someone else and I got confused. However, Tracey was the only blonde in the hostel, including staff. She was very attractive and easily recognisable, and she had not been far away from me. I had an unobstructed view of her.

Am I crazy? Well if I am why did the staff member also hear someone get a drink? I did ask her about it a few days later, and she told me that she was at her mum's, as planned, but while I was talking to her I realised that she was wearing the same clothes as she was when I saw her in the kitchen!

IT TAKES TWO - DERBY

One day in October 2007 I had just come in from Derby College and was sitting in the living room watching television, as I did every day. Nothing was out of the ordinary – or so I thought. Just then my mum walked in the room and she had a surprised look on her face. I asked her what she was doing but she didn't answer me, so I presumed that she either didn't hear me or that she had her mind on something else.

She didn't say anything, but just turned around and walked out of the room. Confused, I decided to follow her to make sure that nothing was wrong. I walked in the direction she went, going though the hallway, her room and her bathroom, but she was nowhere to be seen. I went back into the living room feeling even more confused.

After a little while my brother came in from his mate's house, sat down and we argued over the channels, as most brothers do, then our mum walked in with huge bags of shopping from Tesco. I repeatedly asked her how she had got out, and to my alarm she said she had been gone for about an hour and half. I told her that I had just seen her not five minutes before, but she disagreed and said that I couldn't have done because she wasn't there.

To this day I have no idea how my mum could be in two places at once, but one thing is for sure, it really was very scary!

LOOK-ALIKE - ALVASTON

My dad once told me that when I was younger he had been sitting in the living room of our house in Alvaston, watching TV, when all of a sudden he had seen a little girl who looked like me walk from the kitchen to the bedroom that I shared with my sister. She had been wearing a white night dress and had long, blonde curly hair.

Dad thought that I may have been thirsty, so he got a glass of water and brought it to my bedroom. But when he got there, he saw that my sister and I were both fast asleep.

On another occasion, in the same house, my older cousin David and my father were in the cellar, and they both swear to this day that they saw me again, but I was not even home at the time.

It has been a long time since then and I am 20 now, but since my dad told me that story every time I pass our old house I get the weirdest feeling and chills down my spine.

HIDE AND SEEK - BREADSALL

My friend Sharron has a sister named Tina, and we would often play together in their house in Breadsall Hilltop. Many years ago, when Sharron's mum was pregnant with Tina, she had actually been carrying twins, but tragically one died.

A little while ago Sharron told me a story about something strange that happened when her and Tina were young. They were playing hide and seek in their house, and it was Tina's turn to count. Sharron ran off to hide in the wardrobe, but when she closed the door behind her, there, standing right next to her in the wardrobe, was Tina!

Sharron looked over at her, confused, and said, 'Why aren't you out counting while I hide?' Tina just looked over at Sharron and grinned, then all of a sudden the wardrobe door flung open, and there stood Tina, yelling, 'I found you!' Sharron glanced over to where *Tina* had been sitting, but the figure was gone. Could this have been the ghost of the twin sister that died in the womb, trying to join in her sisters' games?

COUSIN'S MEAN DOUBLE – DERBY

One night my cousin and I were watching TV downstairs in the playroom. We were not supposed to be down there, and at three o'clock my dad caught us. He told us to go straight to bed. Feeling a little guilty, we went straight upstairs and went to sleep. My cousin slept on the top bunk, and I was on the bottom. I was fast asleep until all of a sudden I woke up as my cousin pushed me out of my bed. I looked up at him and yelled, 'What did you do that for? It's like' – I looked at the clock – 'four in the morning!' However, to my surprise, when I looked back at him he was not there. I got out of bed and saw he was still asleep on the top bunk.

Feeling annoyed I woke him up and loudly whispered, 'What was that for? I was asleep, and you just pushed me!'

He groaned back, 'What are you talking about? I didn't even move from up here!'

I was very confused and finally decided that I had just been seeing things and had fallen out of my bed. A little while later, though, my cousin once again pushed me out of bed. This time I didn't even turn my head. I looked up and could clearly see the impression of his body on the top bunk. He was still lying there, sleeping!

I looked back at whoever it was walking into my hallway. The hallway was dark, so I followed. 'Wait!' I yelled, but when I got to the hallway nobody was there, not even my parents. When I woke up the next morning I told my cousin all about it. He was really scared and refused to sleep in my room from then on.

CHAPTER 9

SPIRIT POSSESSION

Spirit possession occurs when the spirit energy is directed at a host object and it uses it to make contact, the outcome of which can be very frightening for all those concerned.

DOLLY NIGHTMARE – DERBY

A while ago my mother went on a day trip to London, and when she was there she bought a doll from a small boutique shop. When she returned she put the doll in my sister's room and that night my sister ran into my mum's room crying and screaming. She said she had had a terrible nightmare.

A few weeks later my mum was home alone cleaning. She was having her own bedroom decorated at the time so she couldn't sleep in it and had to use my sister's room due to the smell of the paint. She had a terrible night and ended up having a bad nightmare just like my sister.

The doll was later placed in my mother's room, rather than my sister's, and as soon as the doll was moved my mum started having nightly nightmares too. After similar events over the next few weeks, my mum decided to get rid of the doll to see if it had anything to do with the nightmares, and to their amazement they immediately ended.

MIRROR, MIRROR, ON THE WALL – SPONDON

When my great-grandma died she left a mirror to me in her will. Because I was still young when she died, the mirror stayed wrapped up in my parents' loft until I left home and rented my first house in Spondon in 1997.

When I moved in my parents came round and brought the mirror with them. It was really beautiful and would probably have been very expensive. It had a solid wood frame and was very heavy and thick, and even though it was very old it had a contemporary feel to it, so I couldn't wait to hang it up on the wall.

No sooner had I put the mirror on the wall, however, I started to see figures in it. At first I was not scared because the woman looked like my great-grandmother, but then I started to see other things in the reflection which were not so pleasant.

I got so paranoid about the mirror that I didn't dare to look into it and so I decided that I had no alternative but to sell it. With the proceeds, I had an old photograph of my great-grandma restored and framed.

SPIRIT OF THE RADIO - DERBY

One night I was asleep in bed, when all of a sudden, at about 3.00am, I woke up to my radio playing. It was on the AM frequency, which I thought was strange, as I never listen to AM radio. I assumed it must have been my flatmate who changed it. I just turned it off, rolled over and went back to sleep, and I did not give it another thought.

However, I woke up again about five minutes later and the radio was blaring next to me. I got up to turn it off, then I realised something that made me freeze in fear. The radio was not playing; it was being tuned. It was flipping back and forth aggressively through the stations.

My eyes widened at the revelation. Something was turning the knob so forcefully the radio was almost moving off the shelf. Hesitantly, I ran up to the radio, grabbed it, ripped the cord out of the wall and smashed it on the wooden floor. I stood above the wreckage, panting with adrenaline and fear. Ever since I have been afraid to tune a radio because the sound it makes brings back horrible memories of that night.

THE CLOWN - STANLEY COMMON

My cousin, who is a lot older than me, used to have a really scary clown doll that she was given as a christening present. One day when I staying with her at her parents' house in Stanley Common, my cousin was annoyed that I had to share her room so she decided to scare me by telling me that the clown moved on its own. I didn't really believe her because I thought it was stupid, and I knew that she had said it because she didn't want to share with me.

Later that night we were in her room, alone. The clown doll had been placed on top of the TV and I thought it was creepy. I was playing with my Barbies instead. My cousin was lying on her bed reading a magazine, and every now and then I would look up to check that the clown was still on top of the TV.

The next time I looked up, however, I saw to my horror that the doll was no longer sitting on the TV. Out of the corner of my eye, I saw a blurry shape next to me on the carpet. I looked to the side of me and there it was – the clown was sitting bolt upright on the floor next to me! I knew that it could not have fallen off the TV because it had been near the back of the unit, so it would have fallen behind. I also knew that there was no way my cousin had moved it because she never got up from the bed.

I shakily told my cousin that it was there, and she looked at me with terror in her eyes. We ran out of the room as fast as we could and closed the door so that the doll would not be able to come out.

THE ROAMING RAG DOLL - DERBY

When my grandma was about 16 she had a room up in the attic of her parents' house. One night she and one of her friends were sitting on the bed and talking, the way teenage girls do. She had a clothes basket in her room, sitting by the door, and on top of it sat a rag doll.

After a while, they heard a noise from the other side of the room. They turned and saw that the doll was on the floor, but they concluded that it had just fallen off. But then, after a few more minutes, they heard the noise again and the doll was closer to the bed. They were slightly nervous now, but went on talking.

Again the sound was heard, which was like a loud 'pop', and this time they jumped as the sound seemed to be coming from right next to them on the bed. They waited there for a few seconds in shock then decided to see what it was. The were stunned to find that the rag doll was now on the bed.

Out of fear, and reflex, they grabbed the curtain rods off the wall, beat the doll with them and threw it out the window. My great-grandma found the doll later that day and asked them about it – but it was simply inexplicable.

THE HAUNTED PAINTING - DERBY

I remember when I was about three years old my family bought the ugliest painting of a woman kneeling down to do something.

CHILLING TALES FROM DERBYSHIRE

I swear that painting seemed to come to life, and the lady would bother me and try to hurt me. She would appear at the end of my bed and talk to me menacingly, but no one else in my family ever saw her.

About three years ago we were gathering things to give away and I sneaked the painting in with the other bits and pieces, and since then I have not been bothered by anything weird!

THE DOLL COLLECTION - DERBY

When I was younger my mum loved to collect these old, spooky looking china dolls. She had about 20 of them. I am not a big fan of dolls because they scare me. I was always afraid to walk past them or even look at them, something which was getting more and more difficult as they seemed to be in every room in the house!

One day my mum was out at work, so no one was home at the time except me. I was walking through our hallway, when I saw the dolls looking straight at me through the gap in the door. All their heads were turned to face me despite the fact that my mother would always pose them to look forward. But what really scared me was the angel doll she had, which I saw crying and praying at the same time later that day. As I stood there, just gawping in terror, another doll that was on display next to her winked at me! I was so scared that I ran out of the room and into my bedroom.

When I told mum about it she thought I was crazy, but after seeing how distressed I was she agreed to get rid of the dolls. I know that I did not imagine it, though, and it has distressed me so much that I still cannot bare to look at china dolls.

TIME TO RISE - SHELTON LOCK

One evening I was staying over at my friend's house in Shelton Lock, and everyone was asleep but us. My friend and I were cleaning up the mess of toys her little cousin had made, when suddenly, seemingly from nowhere, we heard some loud rap music.

We eventually found the source – a clock radio behind a fake plant on the table in the next room. It was flashing midnight on the screen, and ironically one of the song's lyrics was 'I don't know what time it is.' Frightened, we made a point to unplug the clock and turn it off. About five minutes later, however, we heard really soft rock music. We were in complete denial that it was coming from the same unplugged clock radio, so we looked around the whole room. However, we eventually admitted that, to our growing horror, it was coming from there once again. It was again flashing midnight.

My friend then told me that the house was haunted by a ghost who most people thought was her great-grandfather. Apparently, many of the house's guests had had strange things happen to them since his death, like having their feet lifted up in the air or slamming doors, and it seemed that the ghost only played up when there were strangers in the house.

CHAPTER 10

During the 19th century the interest in spiritualism grew rapidly and it seemed that anything which had a spiritual or occult nature would make a sound investment, and this ultimately led to the creation of the Ouija board, a commercial form of 'talking board' which had often been used by spiritualists and psychic mediums.

Two business partners named Elijah Bond and Charles Kennard developed their own version of a spirit board, combining the French and German words for 'yes'. With their head for business and interest in spiritualism, it was not long before the Ouija board was born.

A Ouija board contains letters, numbers and common words such as 'yes', 'no' and 'goodbye'. Users hold a device known as a planchette and supposedly allow the spirit to move it around the board.

Bond and Kennard are historically credited with inventing the modern Ouija board, although it was an employee named William Fuld who took over the commercial production of the official Ouija board. Fuld, however, could not completely prevent competitors from marketing similar boards due to financial restraints, although the name Ouija was a recognised trademark.

On his death, Fuld left an interesting estate, and in 1966 the manufacturing and trademark rights to the game were sold to the Parker Brothers. Today only Parker Brothers can call their product a true Ouija board.

The Ouija board itself is only a medium between the spirit world and the players, although some Ouija board enthusiasts claim the board itself cannot be destroyed. After contacting a willing spirit, players make light contact with the planchette and allow it to move across the board. Individual letters and numbers are often dictated to a non-participant for deciphering. Simple yes-or-no questions can be answered directly.

Many critics of the Ouija board believe the planchette's movements are not caused by spiritual intervention but by involuntary movements created by the players themselves. One or more participants may be forcing the answers, or the players' collective muscle tension could create movement, a phenomenon known as the ideomotor effect. A Ouija board player desperately seeking a spiritual connection with a loved one could also be subconsciously guiding the planchette towards an idealised answer.

There is also a strong religious objection to the Ouija board phenomenon. According to some, Satan could disguise malevolent spirits as the harmless spirit guides sought out by Ouija board users. These evil spirits could use the board as a means of possessing the user's thoughts or to cause personal harm. Prominent Ouija board critics have documented evidence of lives permanently altered following malevolent Ouija board sessions and one of the rules warns against playing the game alone, while another suggests that the spirits must be approached in a specific way to avoid encountering evil impostors and a session should always be ended with the appropriate closure and goodbyes.

I personally have never used a board but I have been called out to many homes in which one has been used in order to spiritually 'clear up', and I would urge anyone who is thinking of using one to proceed with extreme caution as this is certainly not a game.

SPELL...DEATH – REPTON SCHOOL

I went to Repton School in the 1960s. The school, as you may know, is steeped in history and apparently has many ghosts roaming the corridors. One night my friends and I decided to use a Ouija board in some abandoned toilets on the top floor of the building to test out the ghost theories.

Not taking it very seriously, we began to laugh, curse and fool around, but this must have angered whatever spirit was present. We all put our fingers on the glass and chanted for something to come – 'if they dare'. Nothing happened in the first few moments, and just as we were going to quit with snorts of derision, the glass shot suddenly across the board and spelt out d - e - a - t - h. The glass became very hot and moved exceptionally fast. Each one of us fell silent and became very, very afraid when the glass went eerily still. No one said a word and then someone whispered 'are you a bad spirit?' The glass jolted extremely fast to 'Yes'.

At that point we all screamed and left the board as it was. We ran for the door and it slammed shut on us, and although it was simply a push door it was seemingly jammed shut. Then the lights blew and we were deserted in the darkness, crying and screaming for someone to let us out.

The lights began to flash and we were banging uncontrollably on the door as hard as we could. No one came to our aid and we were alone with the terrifying spirit.

The door had a glass panel in the top half, and when the lights suddenly went off we saw a ghostly-white female face pressed close up against the glass, staring in with horrible, angry eyes. At this, one of my friends fainted.

A few seconds later a teacher pushed the door open and said that he had been outside his office down the hallway and had heard screaming. We all ran out of the toilets as fast as we could.

That was the worst experience of my life, and I would strongly advise people not to mess with a Ouija board; it can conjure up anything from the other side. As we did not properly close the board that day, the ghost is probably still roaming.

THE TOOTHY MAN - OSMASTON PARK ROAD, DERBY

One day my friends and I went into my old house on Osmaston Park Road. I knew it was extremely haunted, so we decided to perform a Ouija board séance there.

We began, lights out and candles lit, and asked the ghost we contacted to show itself. He said 'Yes' to that. We looked behind us and the temperature seemed to dip about five degrees. There, in the gloom, we saw an old man in a suit and top hat. As he looked at us, his face became deformed and his jaw dropped and displayed three rows of sharp teeth.

We got up and ran in terror, leaving the board behind. I wonder sometimes if the ghost followed us, as we did not say 'goodbye' on the Ouija board.

ANGRY MAN - DERBY

A few years ago my friend and I were sitting in our friend Laura's room one night after school. We were discussing Ouija, the things we had heard about boards and decided we would have a go with one.

Laura told us that her parents actually owned a board, so she went and got it from a cupboard in her mum and dad's room. We laid the board out, switched off all the lights and lit some candles. I was already scared just thinking about what we were about to do, and it was made worse because Laura only had a few candles, so it was really dark.

We first asked if there was any presence and things like that. We didn't get any answers at first, so we agreed we would try once more and then leave it if noithing happened. We asked again, 'Is there anyone here?'

All of a sudden the glass started to move to 'Yes'. I thought it was my friends messing about, but I could see that they were really scared too, so I was horrified. We asked if the spirit was a female, and it said 'No', then we asked his age, and he said he was around 30. We then asked his name, but he would not tell us, so we asked how he died, but nothing happened. Then, my friend Laura repeated, 'Can you tell us how you died?' At that he got angry and the candles suddenly went out, plunging the room into complete darkness. We could hear objects being thrown across the room and I ran to the switch to turn on the lights, and then everything stopped.

I have never done a Ouija board again, and I never will.

THE BAD BOARD – REPTON

One night at my school, my friend Ivan invited me round to play with a Ouija board at his house in Repton. I asked whether it was safe to play it as I had heard some horror stories and it disturbed me a little when he did not reply, but I joined him nonetheless.

Ivan asked my brother and Janice, his friend, whether they wanted to play too, to make up the numbers. They agreed, and Ivan turned off the lights in the room and lit the candles. He then took out the board and the plastic pointer and started the game.

After a few minutes of silence, we suddenly felt the planchette move. He asked whether it was hungry, and it pointed to 'Yes'. He took out some biscuits that he had brought in to the room and put them beside him, and then the biscuits started to crumble on their own. Everyone closed their eyes and prayed, terrified. Ivan was shocked too and ran away. Since he did not say 'goodbye' to the board, we did it for him and then ran out of the door, vowing never to play with the board again.

NEVER AGAIN – DERBY

My name is Leslie and I am 22 years old. I was born in Nottinghamshire but moved to Derbyshire in 1990. Ever since I could remember I have been interested in ghosts, witches and vampires, you know, all those creepy things. One thing I was always curious about was the Ouija board, but if I ever asked any family members about it they just looked at me with a serious face and told me never to do it.

My first experience with the board was amazing. I was amazed to find something to lead me to the other side, and to talk to my lost loved ones.

I have had many experiences with the board, and I became very addicted to it. There was one particular spirit that would come to the board often by the name of Sally. Over time I learned that Sally was 10 and her father had hanged her in his loft. Sally would sometimes tell me she was good and other times would say she was not. She would also spell out '666' or figures of eight. On one occasion she said that she was sleeping under my friend Gaby's bed and also gave the right description of Gaby's house!

One day I forgot to take the board to school, so my friends and I sat around, talking in the empty school hallway. We started to fool around about Sally, saying, 'Ooh, Sally is gonna get us,' and 'Sally is sleeping under your bed.' We were all just laughing about it really.

The next day I remembered the board, but when we started to use it we noticed that Sally was not acting like her usual self. We asked her if she was mad, and she said 'Yes'. We asked why, and she spelled out 'made fun'. We all freaked out! It was right then and there that I realised it does not matter whether you are playing or not; they are ALWAYS around.

That day I took the board over to Josh's house, who was my boyfriend at the time. He was always bragging about how he was not scared of anything so I asked him if I could keep the board in his house, because my parents no longer wanted to keep it at mine. He agreed, and shortly after I started to play with it in his room with his younger brother Chris. He was not taking it seriously, so I closed the board without saying 'goodbye' and put it away in the cupboard.

That night while Josh was sleeping, he heard footsteps outside his room. Being the brave man that he is, he went to check but saw nothing. He said he felt the area was very cold. He tried to get back to sleep but was awakened by his radio speakers, which were making weird sounds, followed by more footsteps. He was terrified for the first time in his life and did not dare check again in case there was something on the other side of the door.

That morning, when I went to visit him, he told me what had happened and told me he wanted the board out of his house and did not want me to play it anymore.

Four years after not playing, I am still trying to recover from all the evil spirits that I encountered. For anyone who is curious about this message board to the other side, stop your curiosity, because it IS real! And there is absolutely NOTHING good that comes out of the board.

THE AIRBORNE GLASS – DERBY

I had once had one hell of a Ouija board experience. One night my parents went out so my brother, cousin and I decided to play with the board, which we had found under their bed.

We set it up on the dining room table and used a glass as a pointer. We started by asking silly questions and then wanted to know if there were any spirits in the room. The glass started to move and spelled out the name 'Jesse'. I freaked out because there was a guy upstairs, a friend of my dad who was staying with us, with that name. I was so shocked I ended up taking my hand off of the glass. My brother and cousin both kept their hands on the glass and watched it as it slowly moved to the letter 'L', then they removed their hands in shock too. The second they did so the glass shot up into the air, spun around a few times, flew into the middle of the room and landed on the couch. We got so scared we all ran upstairs to see if Jesse was okay.

We opened the door and he was still sleeping. We ran over to him and shook him awake, and then asked him if he was okay. He said he was and wanted to know what was going on. We told him what had happened, and he said he had an uncle with the same name, so we believe it was his uncle in the room talking to us.

We went back downstairs, grabbed the Ouija board, took it outside and poured lighter fluid on it. We set it on fire, and you would not believe what we heard – babies crying, women screaming and people yelling. After the fire died down we looked at the board and incredibly just the edges were burned, so we took it across the street and threw it down the drain.

We all went back into the house, and then I suddenly remembered that if you do not say 'goodbye' to the board, spirits will haunt you.

For the next seven years we had a lot of strange stuff go on in our house. At 6pm every night we heard someone doing the dishes, and when we went to look no one was there. We heard voices and noises around the house. Things got misplaced for days, and then they would reappear. Things got moved to another room, doors opened and closed and other strange things happened too. I finally ended up moving away from the house and I vowed never to touch a Ouija board again in my life.

SAY 'GOODBYE' – UTTOXETER ROAD, DERBY

When I was young my older sister rented a flat in front of a cemetery on Uttoxeter Road. One night I went to stay with her and she decided to play with a Ouija board with one of her friends in the kitchen. I sat in the corner and watched.

About halfway through talking to whatever it was they were talking to, my sister's kitten walked across the board and suddenly started to freak out and hiss and then ran and hid under the sofa. My sister closed the Ouija board up without saying 'goodbye' and rushed to check on the kitten. Her friend was so scared that she decided to leave. After a little while my sister and I went to bed.

I woke up the next morning to find my sister crying. She had found her kitten dead, and its face was disfigured in some sort of odd, twisted manner. She placed it in a shoebox and buried it in the cemetery behind her flat.

After her Ouija board encounter, other strange things started happening. People would get locked in the bathroom from the outside, but there was no lock other than a hook latch on the inside; we would wake up in the morning to find all the cabinets were open and food was all over the worktop and floor; people started to see things walking back and forth in the kitchen and into the bathroom and we would be kept up at night by strange noises coming from downstairs.

One night my brother was staying over at my sister's during a storm. At some point in the night he had been woken up by lightning. He walked into the kitchen and looked out the window to see how bad the storm was. He peered out the window into the cemetery and to his amazement he saw people looking up at him.

My sister finally moved out because she was scared and went to live with my brother. Now when she talks about it I still tell her she should have said goodbye.

'WE'RE OUT HERE' – SOUTH DERBYSHIRE

My friend used to live in a small village in south Derbyshire and one night he decided to have a sleepover.

Just before midnight, when my friend's parents were asleep, he told me he had a Ouija board in the garage. We were curious and went to find it, then set it up in the garage. However, before we even got to ask anything the pointer spelled out the words 'We're out here.'

Of course, at first I thought it was my friend moving the pointer, but when I looked at his face I saw that he was totally pale with fear. We stopped playing right then and I left as soon as I could the next morning.

A few days later my friend called me and said he and his family had seen strange wisps of fog around their house. We were sure that they were the spirits that contacted us that night. After that we never played Ouija again.

PARTY CRASHER - DERBY

A few years ago, my friend Lindsay had a birthday party. The one thing she wanted above anything else was a Ouija board, and to her great pleasure she got one. So that night we all went into the backyard to play with it. We were so excited and more than a little nervous.

We lit a candle and began. Before long we managed to contact the spirit of a young girl who claimed to have been raped in her flat by her father and then killed herself afterwards. I remember it all very clearly, and I remember that the air at the centre of our circle felt uncomfortably warm. Branches were falling in the woods nearby, and we could hear what sounded like rocks being regularly thrown at the car behind us.

We were really stupid when despite our unease we asked the one question we shouldn't have: Are we going to die? The response was 'Yes'. We got up, very frightened, and we bolted for the door. I remember the Ouija board and candle being knocked over in the process. Lindsay's mum's boyfriend told us to finish and we were more than happy to obey.

When we went back outside later, we were shocked to see the candle standing up and lit, and the board set back up with the pointer on 'Goodbye.' We finished our conversation with the girl and said goodbye and immediately the air at the centre of our circle felt cooler.

'SHOULD I? - DERBY

One day my friend and I decided to play the Ouija board. We bought one from a weird shop owned by a lady who always laughed at us, as if we had had our skirts round our feet or something.

I stayed over at my friend's house, and obviously we got the board out. We contacted a few spirits and asked the usual questions: 'What's your name', 'What's your age', etc, but we got no response so we decided to put it away. However, when we tried to put it away, the door on the cupboard we were going to put it into would not close.

We decided to set it up again and straightaway, to our surprise, we managed to contact a spirit. It was really freaky because I was facing a wall which had a mirror almost covering it, and as we were playing I heard a whisper in my ear, saying 'Should I scare your little friend?' I thought to myself I was being silly and was letting the board play with my mind, but then I looked up at the mirror and saw a knife being held to my friend's neck. I screamed and threw the board to the side. My friend asked why I did that and I told her what I saw. We decided we had to continue and I kept hearing the same whisper in my ear. I said out loud, 'Yes', and the moment I said it, the door slammed shut. The light went off but then came back on, and we both turned cold and felt shivers. My friend then said her left cheek felt sore, and when I looked at it there was a giant scratch all the way down it. She then looked in the mirror and screamed. Since then, neither of us have ever played with the board.

TAKEOVER – DERBY

My friend's mum used to live near to the centre of Derby, and one day during her teens she was invited over to an all-night party. One person decided to take a Ouija board to have a bit of fun.

Everybody gathered around and once they had begun one person asked if the ghost would take over somebody, then straightaway my friend's mum started to wail and rock back and forth over and over. Her eyes rolled all the way to the back of her head. Suddenly, all of the lights started to dim as she put her head down. When she looked back up the rest of the guests were shocked to see her smile in a very creepy way. Then everything went back to normal again and her eyes were looking straight ahead and she had relaxed her maniacal smile.

'Hey, this is fun. Let's do it again,' she said. Everyone was giving each other a look as if to say, 'What just happened?' They never did the Ouija board again. Instead, the owner of the board threw it away.

NO WAY! – DERBY

My mother once bought us a Ouija board when I was young about 40 years ago. My sister, two brothers and I thought it was great fun and my mother just thought it was a normal board game. We played it a few times and just asked it random questions which we thought were amusing.

One of my friends and I used to play with the board quite often. A few years later she admitted she was the one pushing the finder just so we could get it over with and do something else, but we did have one interesting experience.

At the time we were going to send our names to a bulletin board so that some servicemen could write to us as a comfort while they were serving abroad. It was a common system then as it was thought that it raised troop morale to receive letters from young women back home. We asked the Ouija board the name of the soldier who would first write to me. The finder started spelling C-A-V-E-N-O-U-G-H. We just giggled about it, but one week later, I received a letter in the mail from a David Cavenough. My friend was with me when I picked up the post and we both screamed in shock!

When my mother found out what the Ouija board really was, she told us she was going to burn it. We did not care much, but each time she told us to go upstairs to find it, it went missing! She finally got hold of it after we had played with it one afternoon, and we never saw it again.

CHAPTER 11
BLOODY MARY STORIES

THE LEGEND OF BLOODY MARY

Most people have probably heard the Bloody Mary legend when they were children, listening to spooky ghost stories around the campfire or on Halloween. It originates from England but the story has travelled widely, with each country having their own variation on the legend.

It is widely believed that the evil witch can be summoned by chanting 'Bloody Mary' three times into a mirror in a darkened room at the stroke of midnight, although the number of times 'Bloody Mary' needs to be called seems to vary, with three and 13 seeming to be the most popular number. The bathroom is also the most popular setting to test out the legend, but other dark rooms also seem applicable.

The game is often a test of courage, as it is said that if Bloody Mary is summoned she will proceed to kill whoever calls her name in an extremely violent way after driving the person insane.

Who Bloody Mary really was remains a mystery. While there are many versions of this story, most accounts point to a witch named Mary Worth, who was burned at the stake many years ago and now returns to take her revenge.

THE STORY OF MARY WORTH

Mary Worth lived deep in a forest in a cottage and sold herbal remedies for a living, as did many of the so-called mediaeval 'witches'. People living in the town nearby called her Bloody Mary and said she must be a witch because she could heal people with her herbs. No one dared cross the old crone for fear that their cows would go dry, their food-stores would rot away before winter, their children became sick with fever or any number of other terrible things that an angry witch could do.

After a while the little girls in the village began to disappear, one by one. No one could find out where they had gone and grief-stricken families searched the woods, the local buildings and all the houses and barns, but there was no sign of them. A few brave souls even ventured out to Bloody Mary's home in the woods to see if the witch had taken them, but she denied any knowledge of the disappearances. Still, it was noted that her haggard appearance had changed. She looked younger and more attractive, and the neighbours were suspicious, but they could find no proof that the witch had taken their daughters.

Legend has it that one night the daughter of the miller rose from her bed and walked outside, following an enchanting sound that no one else could hear. The miller's wife had a toothache and was sitting up in the kitchen treating the tooth with an herbal remedy when her daughter left. She screamed for her husband and followed the girl out of the door. The miller came running in, dressed in his nightshirt, and together they tried to restrain the girl, but she kept breaking away from them and heading out of town.

The desperate cries of the miller and his wife woke the other villagers, who came to assist the frantic couple. Suddenly, a sharp-eyed farmer gave a shout and pointed towards a strange light at the edge of the woods. A few townsmen followed him out into the field and there, to their horror, they saw Bloody Mary standing beside a large oak tree, holding a magic wand that was pointed towards the miller's house. They saw that she was glowing with an unearthly light as she cast her evil spell upon the miller's daughter.

The townsmen grabbed their guns and pitchforks and ran towards the witch. When she heard the commotion, Bloody Mary broke off her spell and fled into the woods. One far-sighted farmer had loaded his gun with silver bullets in case the witch ever came after his daughter, and now he took aim and shot at her fleeing figure. The bullet hit Bloody Mary in the hip and she fell to the ground. The angry townsmen leapt upon her and carried her back into the field, where they built a huge bonfire and burned her at the stake.

As she burned, Bloody Mary screamed a terrible curse at the villagers. She shrieked through the pain that should anyone mention her name aloud before a mirror, she would send her spirit as revenge for her terrible death. With that, she finally succumbed to the flames and died in agony. When she was dead, the villagers went to her house in the wood and found the unmarked graves of the little girls the evil witch had murdered. She had used their blood in spells to make herself young again.

From that day to this, anyone foolish enough to chant Bloody Mary's name three times before a darkened mirror will summon the vengeful spirit. It is said that she will tear their body to pieces and rip their soul from their mutilated corpse. The souls of these unfortunate victims will burn in torment as Bloody Mary once was burned, and they will be trapped forever in the mirror.

So be warned!

Something about Mary - Derby

One night my parents went out to see a film at the cinema and I had my friend over to stay at our house. We were both 15 at the time. As the evening went on we became very bored. There was nothing on the TV, and as we felt in a mischievous mood we decided to play 'Bloody Mary'. I had heard the legend only a few days before and so I was itching to try it out.

We made our way to the bathroom and chanted her name into the mirror three times, just as I had heard we were supposed to. We didn't get that scared at first, but then we started hearing noises. We left the bathroom as it suddenly started to feel very creepy in there and just then the phone rang. I picked it up but there was nobody on the other end, then the windows started vibrating and we had no idea why. We started to feel very frightened, so we decided to go outside, then all of a sudden we saw a lady standing in the shadows by the house. Before we had chance to speak she said to us, 'Your mum told me to wait here till 3.00am.'

I said, 'Who are you?'

'Mary,' she replied.

'Okay, Mary,' I said, thinking that she was a friend of my mum's, 'come on in.' She followed us into the house, where she started to act all weird. She said that she wanted some pictures of me, which I thought was really odd, but I still believed she was my mum's friend and let her have them.

After she took the pictures, she looked at me said, 'I have to go.'

'You have to stay till 3.00am and it's only 9.30pm,' I pointed out, now completely confused as to who the hell she was.

She simply replied, 'Thanks, it's okay.'

The following day I told my mum about our strange visit and asked her why she sent Mary to our place. To my surprise, she had no idea what I was talking about.

Slowly, over the next few weeks, bad things started to happen to my friend and I. We came to believe that she was not just anyone who visited that night – she was Bloody Mary. I was really scared, so one night not long after when my parents went out again, my friend and I called her again. She came and admitted that she knew bad things were happening to us. Terrified, I asked her, 'What do you want?'

'Stop calling out my name,' she replied, 'and I'll stop bothering you.'

After that night I never mentioned her name to anyone. Whoever reads this story, please do not play such a game – you might get more than you bargained for.

BLOODY MARY SCRATCHES – DRAYCOTT

When I was 10 my family and I moved to a house in Draycott. Some older kids had introduced my friend Alli and I to Bloody Mary, but we thought that it was a load of rubbish.

One night we were having a sleepover at Alli's house, and we decided to call Bloody Mary just for kicks. We went into the bathroom, which had blue tiles, a mirror all along wall above the double sink and a tiled bathtub with a clear shower curtain. It was quite a large room.

Alli and I wrote 'Bloody Mary' on the mirror, switched off the light and turned around three times, as we had been told, while repeating her name. Then when we looked into the mirror in the pitch black we saw in the reflection a bathroom drenched in blood, a bath filled with blood and a ghostly body.

Alli and I screamed in terror. All of a sudden we felt like we were being bitten and scratched all over our bodies. Eventually we managed to turn the light back on, and we were amazed to find everything back to normal, except, that is, for the fact that we both had scratches all over our arms and faces and I had a very clear bite mark on my shoulder.

We never ever played Bloody Mary again.

CHAPTER 12
ELEMENTALS

Elementals is the name given to nature spirits such as fairies and elves. They are all connected to the natural elements and each different type is said to resonate with the five main elements of air, water, earth, wood and metal.

It is interesting to note that although I have not included many stories of elementals in this book, throughout history there have been many stories and pictures about such little people, and this fascinates me because if they are merely legends and myths, as most scholars lead us to believe, then why have their stories stood the test of time and why have they been told throughout many continents? Makes you think doesn't it?

A PICNIC TO REMEMBER – ELVASTON CASTLE

One beautiful summer's day I decided that I would take my children to Elvaston Castle for a picnic. I soon had everything ready and off we went for a fun day out.

When we got there we found it was very busy, and as my children wanted to play with the ball they had packed we decided to explore the grounds to find a more secluded spot. We walked along the side of the old church, through a grassy area with a Monkey tree at the end, and then we came to a stretch of grass that was perfect.

As I started to lay out the food, the children played with the football and I marvelled at how perfect the day was. My children had only just started playing, when my youngest son kicked the ball into a hedge. As the children walked over to retrieve it, the ball was suddenly thrown back onto the grass, so the children continued to walk forward to thank whoever had thrown it back, however they found only dense bushes and no one in sight.

The game resumed and soon the ball was kicked back in the bushes, and yet again the ball was seemingly thrown out of the bush with some force. Puzzled, I got up to investigate myself and could not believe what I saw in the bushes: sitting there, right in front of me, in the middle of a bush was a tiny creature about 6 inches tall with a shrivelled face; it looked like a little old man with spindly legs and pointy ears. It took one look at me and scuttled off into the bushes, obviously as scared as I was.

I returned to our picnic and packed it away as quick as I could, not breathing a word of what I had seen to the children as I didn't want to scare them.

To this day I can clearly remember the ugly little chap and I'm relieved to say that I have never seen anything like it since.

FAIRIES AT THE BOTTOM OF THE GARDEN – CROSSHILL

When I was a small child, my grandmother used to live in a big house surrounded my gardens near Crosshill in Derbyshire. It was an imposing house with a lot of tiny windows covering it, which always seemed to me to be rather too small for the stature of the house and out of proportion in some way.

I dearly loved my grandmother and loved to spend as much time with her as I could as she always seemed to have an abundance of patience, which was something that my own parents were lacking, and so I looked forward to my time with her and savoured every moment.

My grandmother taught me everything from darning and cookery to fishing and gardening. There seemed to be nothing that she couldn't do, and thankfully she had the time to pass on her skills to me, which I, in turn, passed on to my own children.

Nothing ever seemed to faze my grandmother and she was well known for speaking her mind and telling the truth.

One day I arrived at my grandmother's house to find her out in the garden, tending and pruning her beautiful array of rose bushes. As soon as she saw me she welcomed me with open arms and told me that today she would teach me to prune and grow the best roses in Derbyshire, and she then proceeded to hand me a pair of rusty 'snippets', as she used to call them.

'I saw something remarkable this morning Rosie,' she told me, almost in a whisper. 'Right there under the apple tree...I saw a little man with wings.'

I stood there with my mouth gaping wide open. 'Was he a fairy?' I asked, nervously.

'I think he must have been. He had a greyish tinge to his cloth jacket and silver wings, but he was not pretty like the fairies in the books, he was ugly with big ears,' my grandmother continued.

My grandmother was not a woman to joke or lie, so I decided that she must have been telling me the truth.

We worked all day on the roses, snipping off the best blooms and carrying them into the house to make floral arrangements, while dead-heading the others and throwing them on the compost heap next to the apple tree in the corner. I had just started to walk over to the compost heap when something caught my eye. It was small and seemed to dart across between the foot of the apple tree and the compost heap. It only stood about six inches tall and had what looked like a sack for a shirt. It had clear wings, very similar to that of a dragonfly, and had an extremely pointy face. It was just as my grandmother had described it.

I stared, frozen to the spot, and it was not long before my grandmother came to see why I wasn't moving. As soon as she approached me, she saw what I was looking at and gently placed her hand on my shoulder, almost relieved that I too had witnessed it. I think she found it reassuring that her mind was still quite intact!

My grandmother and I stood there for what seemed like a lifetime, but in reality it could only have been about five minutes, watching the strange little man run between the tree and compost heap, and then he turned, noticed we were watching him and as quick as a flash he darted underneath the compost heap and we never saw him again.

We walked back to the house together in silence, both completely stunned. We only found our voices when we got back to the kitchen and my grandmother had poured us both some lemonade.

'I don't know why we saw that little man today but I do know that we must not tell anyone, because if we do they may want to have a look for themselves and frighten the little man off,' my grandmother said to me with a reassuring smile. So that is what we did. I never told another living soul until my grandmother's death many years later, but even then, when I retold the story nobody believed me and so I simply stopped telling anyone, but I know that what my grandmother and I saw that day was very real and I cherish the fact that we were able to witness it together.

CHAPTER 13
SHADOW PEOPLE

It is thought that shadow people are usually attracted to one particular person or location, but the reasons for this are unknown. They are often reported as dark silhouettes of a human shape, generally male, that prefer to watch someone unseen and flee the moment they are noticed. Their personalities range wildly from shy to downright nasty, but it is my belief that shadow people are not evil or demonic, they simply represent a different configuration pattern than the previously documented orbs, vortices and ectoplasmic swirls and vapour which are the shapes of spirit energy.

It has also been reported that they have a tendency to feed on a person's fear, which can lead to their behaviour being erratic. So if you see one the best thing to do is stay calm.

DEMON IN THE HALL – KEDLESTON ROAD

When I was a student at Derby University I rented a room in a house just off Kedleston Road, and while it was not the best of houses, the five lads that I shared with made it our home.

One Friday night all my housemates were heading into Derby for a few drinks, but as I didn't have any money and had the biggest essay to write I decided that I should stay in and get it finished so I could spend the rest of the weekend with my girlfriend.

I was alone in the house and was in my room studying when, out of the corner of my eye, I saw what looked like a black shadow walk out of the wall and straight into another. I looked over to where I thought I had seen it but there was nothing there. I just told myself that it was something in my head and got back to work.

Not too long after that I saw another shadowy black figure come out of the wall. This time when I looked over into the hallway I saw that it had not gone away. It was just floating in the hallway, seemingly staring at me. I was so scared that I tried to get up, but I couldn't move. It was as if I were paralysed. I was petrified as it began to move towards me.

Suddenly I found that I could move, so I started throwing things at the figure, but to my horror the objects just went right through it. As it got closer I began to scream, but no sound came out.

Finally I saw a cross on the table that my grandma had given to me before I started university. I looked at the figure and threw the cross at it and the shadow just backed up and disappeared into the wall. After it left, I was suddenly able to move and talk. The whole episode was very scary, like I was in some sort of horror movie, and I was thankful that it never happened again.

When my mates arrived home I told them all about what had happened and one admitted that he had seen something that matched my description two nights before but didn't want to say anything because he didn't think anyone would believe him. I wish he had said something, because I might have thought twice about staying in the house on my own that night!

SHADOWS DO NOT FEEL PAIN - MACKWORTH

One day I was at my grandpa's house in Mackworth, and I was all alone. My family had all gone to Derby so I had to look after my grandpa's dog while they were out as they would not be back home until late.

When they all left it was already getting dark. It was about 9.00pm and I decided to go straight to bed as I was really tired, but no sooner had I drifted off to sleep, I woke up for no reason at all. I looked around the room to see what had caused me to wake, then when I looked towards the stairs I could see what looked like a figure in the shadows. I grabbed one of my baby sister's toys that were kept in the room and got it into a position to hit the intruder.

Thinking that it was a burglar, I slowly crept out of bed and over to where I thought the figure was standing. I swung the toy in my hand (I think it was a wooden building block) as hard as I could at the shadow, hoping that I could scare them into leaving. To my horror, however, my hand went straight through the shadow, which then floated away from where I was standing and disappeared straight through a wall.

PRESENCE - DERBY

One night I woke up very suddenly because I thought I heard my door handle. At first I just thought it was my other half coming back from work, as he worked at the railway station and sometimes was able to finish his nightshift early. As I turned over, half asleep, I saw a light.

The next thing I knew I couldn't move. My body was shaking and my feet were rising off the bed. I tried to scream, but all I could hear was buzzing in my ears and no sound came out.

I turned and reopened my eyes as I was scared stiff. Then, I began to feel terrified as I saw a dark shadow walking around my room – it was certainly not human. After that I hid under my covers and remained there until my partner came home.

PICTURE THIS! – DERBY

One Friday night when I was walking down the stairs to do some washing, all of a sudden a picture fell off the wall in front of me. I was surprised by it but didn't really give it another thought.

When I had finished putting the washing on I went back to the stairs to try and re-hang the picture. I picked up the picture and looked at the two nails that were meant to be holding it up. On further investigation, I found that the nails were both rigid in the wall and I could see no reason why it had fallen.

Suddenly, as I stood there, I felt a cool breeze rush past me, and when I turned around there was a dark figure by the wall. I screamed, dropped the empty laundry basket and ran upstairs as fast as I could. My heart was beating out of my chest as I looked behind me and saw that the shadow seemed to be following me up the stairs. The dark shadow grew in size as it chased me and I swear I heard a horrible hissing sound coming from it.

I hid under my bedclothes for a while and thankfully didn't see it again.

A HEAVY BREATHER – DERBYSHIRE

Throughout my childhood I often saw shadow people, from the corner of my eye. Generally I gave little thought to them because I was used to them until, when I was 11, I had a very frightening encounter with one. It was the first of three incidences I have had of shadow ghosts actually interacting with me as opposed to me just seeing them.

I woke up in the night and lay in bed for a little while, just staring up at the ceiling. I was completely awake and thinking about school and how much I was not looking forward to the end of the summer holiday. I was about to drift back to sleep when all of a sudden I heard heavy breathing coming from the other side of the room. After hearing it, I immediately sat up and turned to look towards the sound. And there, standing in front of one of the windows, I saw a black silhouette in the corner of my bedroom. I couldn't see any eyes, but somehow I knew it was looking at me while it breathed.

My first thought was that it was my brother trying to scare me, so I said to the figure 'Get out, you're not funny.' There was no reaction, it just continued to stare and breathe. So again I spoke, saying, 'You! Get out! You're not funny,' but again there was no reaction.

I became quite frustrated and angry at that point because my brother wouldn't stop, so I took my pillow and screamed 'GET OUT', at which point I threw the pillow at the figure. To my surprise the pillow sailed right through it, and as soon as I had thrown it the figure disappeared, but just after the pillow hit the window behind it, the figure re-appeared.

Upon seeing that happen, I was up and out of my bedroom in a flash, screaming bloody murder. I ran to my parents and told them what I had seen. They took me back into my room and turned on the lights and saw that the pillow was over in the corner beneath the window, but there was no figure there. My parents insisted that I had been dreaming, no matter how much I argued that I had been wide awake.

The incident frightened me so badly that it completely changed my sleeping pattern for two years. I could only sleep with my head at the end of the bed so I could watch the corner where the figure had appeared and I also refused to sleep if the lights were off.

Now that I am an adult I am no longer afraid of what I saw that night. I tend to think that the shadow person was not there to do me any harm, because I never really felt frightened by it.

WHAT THE HELL? - DERBY

One day I was sitting in my friend's dining room and was on her computer, when all of a sudden I heard the sound of footsteps upstairs. I thought it was impossible, since we were both downstairs and there was nobody else at home. At first I just put it down to her two cats, but then I remembered that they were on the settee. A little puzzled, I went to check on them out of curiosity. I had just walked into the lounge when all of a sudden I saw the shadow of a man dressed in dark clothing rush down the stairs and out through the front door.

I screamed and found that I was rooted to the spot, totally unable to move. I never saw it again, but I know what I saw that night. I never believed in anything paranormal before then, but the realism of that shadowy figure sure changed my mind!

LOOK OUT! – HILTON

In 2007 I moved into a beautiful one-bedroomed house in Hilton. I was happy and relaxed in my new home, but that happiness soon turned into fear.

I was home alone one day, watching TV, when suddenly I felt a tap on my shoulder. I looked behind me, but nothing was there. I felt it again; it was a hard, unfriendly tap. Finally, I stood up to look around but found nothing.

As I sat back down, I was horrified to see a shadow appear to float around the living room, then it stopped and seemed to be looking at something – it was another shadow! They turned towards me and then slowly faded away. I was stunned, and frozen with fear. I decided that it would be a good idea to get out of the house for a few hours, and when I came back, there was writing on the wall made by a marker pen. It said 'Look out!' It took me a long time to make it out as the writing was very much a scrawl, and it definitely had not been there before as I had repainted that room first when I moved in.

Weird things have happened since then, but I have learned to ignore them; however, those shadowy figures have never left as they still reappear every now and again.

THE DARKER SIDE OF THE DOOR – DERBY

I was at my girlfriend's house one night and we were watching TV. At around midnight, we kept hearing some strange noises coming from the hallway next to her room.

It sounded as though the floor was creaking, as if someone was walking through there. We turned to look at each other as we realised that everyone else in the house had been in bed for hours. We ignored the noise in the end and went to bed about an hour later, but as soon as I fell asleep, I awoke to the same noises. This time, as I listened, I realised that the steps were getting closer to us. I was so scared I lay under the covers motionless, my eyes barely open enough to peep and see.

All of a sudden it got very quiet and the air went still. Then the door to the room, which was locked, started to open! I watched amazed as a dark shadow figure walked into the room as if searching for something and then walked right back out.

I asked everyone in the house the next morning if they had walked into the room, and to my surprise they all said that they hadn't.

FROST BITE – BORROWASH

One day a few years ago I was at home with my best friend, Leon. We had known each other forever and been best friends for a long time, since we both attended Ashbrook Primary School in Borrowash. We were home alone for some time as my parents had gone out for a dinner date. We had been watching TV, when suddenly my friend started hearing noises that sounded as if they were coming from the spare bedroom. We nervously debated whether we should go up and investigate or not until we finally plucked up the courage to check it out. I had always been a little braver and stronger than Leon, so I led the way. The spare room was up the stairs and the first room on the right. We got to the door and looked at each other, and I put my hand out as I nervously gripped the doorknob and tried to turn it. It felt very cold and was diffiult to turn. Then, finally, I got it open.

There in front of me was a figure in the room. It was dark and not very tall, and it seemed as if its left arm was very big. It was right in front of me and I froze with fear. I tried to scream as it moved closer and put its hand on my chest. It was freezing cold.

Just then my chest started to hurt very badly. I staggered around a little, but I couldn't seem to get away then I felt something hit my cheek. I raised my hand to feel what it was and I was horrified to see there was blood dripping from a deep cut on my face. I frantically yelled to Leon to do something. He ran up to the door and slammed it shut and the thing suddenly vanished. I fell back and hit the wall and I guess I must have lost consciousness. I eventually woke up downstairs near the door; Leon must have dragged me there. I looked at my chest and saw that there was a spot of blood where the thing had put its hand. I quickly wiped it off. My chest was hurting terribly and I tried to get up, but I couldn't. I asked Leon what happened.

'I – I don't know,' Leon said. 'You're bleeding.' I touched my face and sure enough it was still bleeding.

Thankfully, nothing else happened after that. When my parents got home, we told them what had happened and we moved down the street within a month. Leon and I didn't even dare look at that house ever again.

CHAPTER 14

There isn't one, I'm just wildly superstitious!